THE GRADUAL SPELLING PROGRAMME

Structured, simple and stress free

Anya Bensberg

About the Author

Anya Bensberg BSc (LSE) MA (UCL), MEd (CCU), DipSpLD (Northampton), APC. Anya has taught and assessed many children and adults with dyslexia throughout her career. She is currently Deputy Head (Academic) at St Edmund's School Canterbury. St Edmund's School is an independent co-educational day and boarding school for ages 3-18.

Anya's contact details are aeb@stedmunds.org.uk

Acknowledgements

Various people have contributed in some way to this work, not least the many pupils I have taught. The idea and broad outline of the book originated in discussions with Sue Whitehead. The material includes examples drawn from various resources used by the Inclusion Department at Bishop Stopford School, Northamptonshire. Special thanks are due to Frances Ward for editing the text in a way that was both meticulous and creative.

Contents

Introduction

Dyslexia is primarily a difficulty affecting the skills involved in accurate word reading and spelling. The latest research says that dyslexia should be viewed as a continuum; the difficulties vary in severity and can occur across a range of intellectual abilities.

Many published spelling programmes assume that learners have a basic knowledge of vowel and letter sounds and can recognise common blends. The Gradual Spelling Programme teaches these basics from the beginning, using a structured approach. It is aimed at learners with persistent dyslexic difficulties who need grounding in the basics before moving on to look at the more sophisticated letter patterns.

The Gradual Spelling Programme offers the opportunity to start at the very beginning, and establish the building blocks upon which further learning can rest. Teaching structured spelling, even at the most basic levels, encourages independence by showing learners how to break words down into their component parts.

The resources and suggested teaching methods have been designed for any learner from age 5-upwards.

Theory

The normal pattern of learning to read and write may be described as follows. The first stage is the logographic stage, recognising and naming whole words, e.g. ('It says *Tesco*!') in the same kind of way you might recognise a car ('It's a Landrover!'). The second stage involves recognising that letters or combinations of letters (phonemes) represent the sounds in known spoken words. The final stage is when the link between word meanings and spellings becomes instantaneous. There is some discussion as to whether spelling is a natural extension to reading, although agreement does exist that spelling is a more difficult task than reading. Dyslexic learners do not absorb the skills of written language the same way as others and benefit from explicitly being taught these skills.

Many learners with persistent dyslexic difficulties cannot get past the first stage of recognising and naming whole words. They may be able to read and spell from their sight vocabulary, but do not make links between letters, letter combinations and sounds. That is why the GSP is very visual and focuses on learning to spell 10 key words for each sound.

Teaching phonemes is an important part of any spelling programme: letters and phoneme patterns form the basis for the scheme of work detailed in chapters 3-6. The introduction of each teaching point in the gradual spelling programme builds on the logographic style to which the dyslexic learner with persistent difficulties is accustomed, as it involves the learner recognising and naming a few key whole words (containing the phoneme pattern). The aim is that the learner will read, spell and ultimately, remember these words in context of the phoneme(s). A learner at the logographic stage should achieve well on this programme.

How to use this book

The Purpose of a Miscue

The programme can be used to teach an individual learner or a class. Before starting on the programme it is useful to perform a miscue on your learner(s). This has two advantages: to inform your teaching by giving an overview of the learners needs, enabling them to choose lesson content that is relevant, and to provide a means to evaluate the learner(s) progress on the programme by setting a baseline spelling accuracy score which should show an improvement.

Miscue: Alphabet

Before starting the Gradual Spelling Programme it is essential to test pupils' alphabet knowledge. This can be done by using a tactile alphabet, such as a wooden alphabet or the cut out alphabet provided, which can be photocopied onto card. Use the alphabet with the student and check their knowledge on the areas below. Remember the purpose of this is to check prior knowledge, not to teach, so if the student is struggling they should be reassured, ("This is not a test. We're doing this, to see what I need to teach you.") Then move onto the next area on the checklist.

Miscue Alphabet Checklist

Is the learner able to

     a)   Sequence the alphabet?

     b)   Identify vowels?

     c)   Know letter names (e.g. a is said ā or ay)

     d)   Know letter sounds (e.g. a in fat is ă or ah)

Ability to at least partially understand these areas is important before embarking onto other parts of the programme. If your student struggles it is essential to work through the areas using the alphabet worksheets provided.

Miscue: Spelling

Purpose

The miscue is essentially a spelling test to enable the teacher to help each learner effectively. It is important to explain to the learner that they are not expected to be able to spell all the words ("I would like to know which spellings you find easy and which are harder.")

Process

The process of testing should be started by giving lined paper to each learner. Ask them to write the words in a list down the page. Then slowly read each word. You should say the word, then say the word in a sentence (e.g. "cut, I cut my foot"), then say the word again. This puts the word into context without overloading the working memory. Learners may have up to ten seconds to spell each word but may not need this long.

Obtaining the Miscue

Mark the test by using a highlighter to mark the problematic words. Then mark off the corresponding spelling patterns on your photocopied list. Use the crosschecker to help. Once the spelling patterns have been marked off you will have a clear view of the areas requiring intervention. If you find your learner is secure on a vowel or blend you probably won't teach it.

Evaluating success

Count the correct number of spellings your learner has managed and give a score out of 33. From this you can work out the learner's percentage of accuracy. The miscue can be used to check progress, alongside other standardised spelling tests. Keep the test results somewhere safe, as you should retest your student around every 6 months to check their progress.

Structure of Programme

The aim is that after 2 lessons students are able to read and spell some words containing the phoneme at sentence level. This is assessed by marking the accurate spelling of a number of words containing the phoneme which are given within dictated sentences.

It is important that learners use their visual, auditory and kinaesthetic skills during lessons. One student may be particularly strong in one area and you may later adapt activities accordingly. It is important to cover all three when teaching a group. All learners on the programme will probably need to use a variety of activities to reinforce learning. These activities are designed to be fun and are broken down into simple steps. The idea is to break learning down as much as possible in order to make success attainable for the learner. The programme is designed to spend two lessons on each phoneme, but some learners may need a little more or less time.

The phoneme is first introduced visually and at word level. The aim of the first lesson is that learners read and spell words containing the phoneme. Activities are fun, and focus around reading and spelling target words in a multisensory way. Prior learning is tested and then built upon during the second lesson. The aim is that by now students are able to read and spell the phoneme within sentences.

The final assessment of learning for each phoneme is towards the end of the second lesson when the teacher reads out sentences containing the phoneme to the learner. To build working memory, the learner must repeat back each sentence in turn before writing it down. The dictated sentences are then marked by the teacher, who gives a success score based on the number of words containing the phoneme and spelt correctly.

Summary of lesson structures

Lesson 1

   a) Students read target words

   b) Reinforcement activities at word level

   c) Spell words at word level

   d) Reinforcement game

3

Lesson 2

    a) Use target words or game to reintroduce target words

    b) Students spell words at word level

    c) Reinforcement activities at sentence level

    d) Dictation sentences

The Resources

The book contains a variety of multisensory and interactive resources which are designed to make learning fun. The resources include a mixture of worksheets which may be photocopied.

The resources listed below will work best when photocopied onto card or laminated.

Word cards – it is suggested that the word cards are shown to learners when introducing a new sound. Word cards may be read aloud along with discussion on word meanings.

Matching cards – the pages containing words from word cards and corresponding pictures may be used as matching or pairs games.

'Climb the ladder' game – the board contains two ladders and the word cards are designed to be cut out and used along with the game.

'Cross the river' game – the board works best when enlarged to A3 and used with 2 counters. It can be photocopied for single use or laminated and for multiple use.

Connect 3 game – the board can be photocopied for single use or laminated and used multiple times

High Frequency Words

Some (not all) dyslexic learners struggle with spelling high frequency words. The Gradual Spelling Programme does not specifically address high frequency words, but it is still possible to incorporate them into your teaching while using this programme. The dictation sentences used to test understanding of each sound include high frequency words. If your learner(s) are spelling high frequency words incorrectly in their dictation sentences it is suggested that you address this. You can a) ask the learner to write the high frequency word out in their book 3 times then, b) create a card for the word (similar to the word cards used for each new sound). Recap using the high frequency word cards at the beginning or end of each lesson and test your learner's spelling of them frequently. Since many high frequency words are irregular (cannot be sounded out) learners often benefit from learning them using memory hooks such as mnemonics, which can also be incorporated onto cards. One example of a mnemonic to learn a high frequency word, said, might be **s**illy **a**nimals **i**n **d**ustbins or **S**ally-**A**nn **is d**izzy.

Miscue Spelling Test

Instructions

Read each word out once, put it into a sentence that makes sense (e.g. I cut my hand) and then read it again. Allow students up to 10 seconds to spell each word.

1. cut
2. hot
3. tap
4. peg
5. fit
6. god
7. bin
8. met
9. jam
10. slug
11. click
12. bash
13. silk
14. string
15. mist
16. snip
17. clasp
18. chin
19. gland
20. splash
21. plump
22. strip
23. trot
24. drop
25. flag
26. ramp
27. grand
28. pram
29. spin
30. crab
31. glow
32. blunt
33. stink

Gradual letter order

	CVC
jam, tap	a
peg, met	e
fit, bin	i
hot, god	o
cut	u
	S BLENDS
stink, mist	st
slug	sl
spin, clasp	sp
snip	sn
shin, splash	sh
	R BLENDS
drop	dr
trot	tr
crab	cr
pram	pr
grand	gr

	L BLENDS
gland, glow	gl
clasp, click	cl
blunt	bl
flag	fl
plump	pl
	END BLENDS
stink	nk
gland, grand	nd
string	ng
blunt	nt
plump, ramp	mp
melt	lt
silk	lk
	TRIPLE BLENDS
splash	spl
string, strip	str
	CONSONANT DIAGRAPHS
splash, bash	sh
chin	ch
click	ck

The Alphabet

Why is the Alphabet important?

Join each box to the matching picture.

To find a word in
the dictionary

To understand
the register

To find a book in
the library

To vote

To use a filing
cabinet

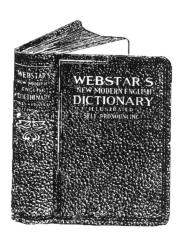

Finished? Do you know the alphabet?

Write as much as you can below.

A B C

D E F

G H I

8

J K L

M N O

P Q

R S T

U V W

X Y Z

Sequencing

Know the first bit of the alphabet? Join the dots below.

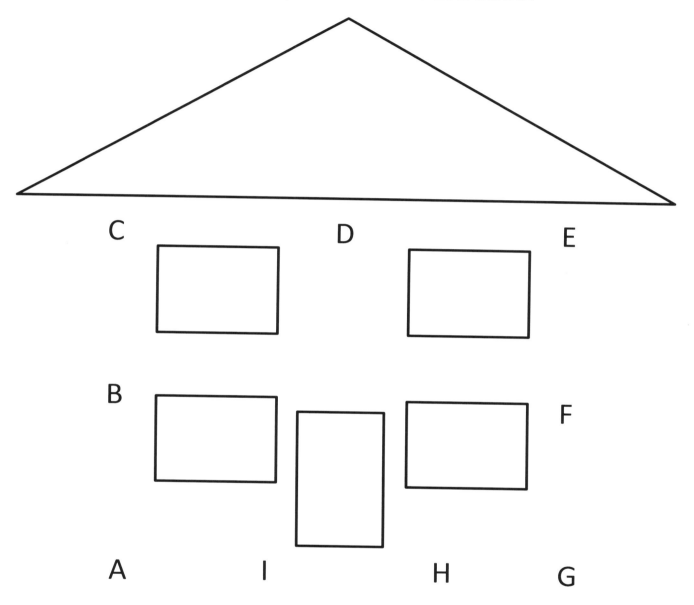

ABCDEFGHIJKLMNOPQRSTUVWXYZ

Know half of the alphabet? Join the dots below.

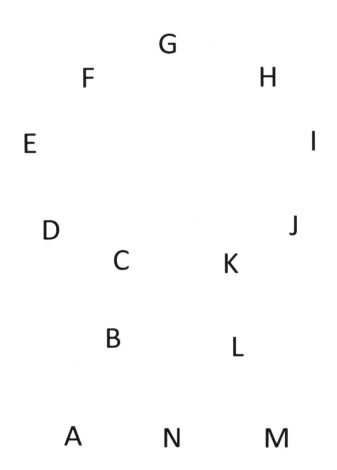

ABCDEFGHIJKLMNOPQRSTUVWXYZ

Know almost all the alphabet? Join the dots below.

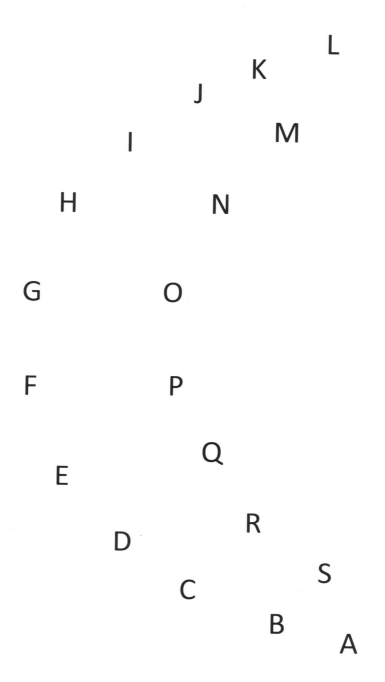

ABCDEFGHIJKLMNOPQRSTUVWXYZ

Know the whole alphabet? Join the dots below.

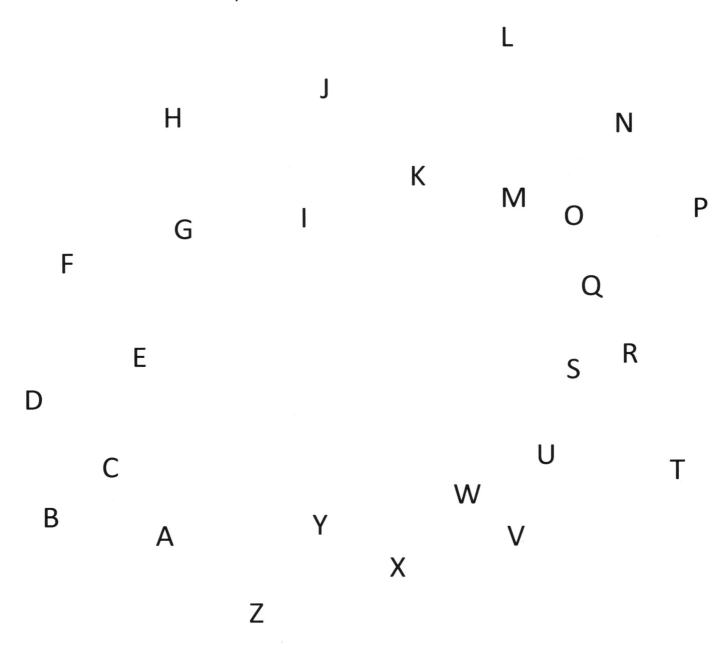

ABCDEFGHIJKLMNOPQRSTUVWXYZ

Alphabet cards to enlarge, laminate and cut out. Place the cards into order. The learner must then read each card out before moving to the next. This activity helps with alphabet sequencing skills.

A B -	B C -	C D -	D E -	E F -
F G -	G H -	H I -	I J -	J K -
K L -	L M -	M N -	N O -	O P -
P Q -	Q R -	R S -	S T -	T U -
U V -	V W -	W X -	X Y -	

Introducing... the vowels

Vowels are important because there is at least one vowel in every word.

Show you can find the vowels by colouring them in when you read the words below.

Now write your name and highlight the vowels

Which words have long and short vowel sounds?

Write the word in the correct box

Ō	ŏ

oblong   over   open   orange   own

ā	ă

apple   alien   adder   able   add

ē	ĕ

egg   evil   every   enter   e-bay

ī	ĭ

in   ice   igloo   island   I

ū	ŭ

up   union   university   under   us

Extension

We also get long vowel sounds in the middle of words. Read each word and see if you can work out if the vowel (in bold) makes a long or short sound.

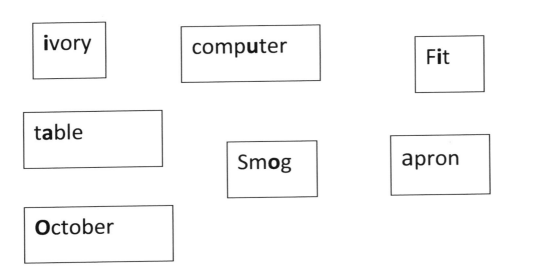

ivory   comp**u**ter   F**i**t

t**a**ble   Sm**o**g   **a**pron

October

ă

mat

tap

fan

man

bag

hat

cat

rat

pan

map

Read each word, then draw picture in the square above

tap This is a _ _ _	**mat** This is a _ _ _	**man** This is a _ _ _
hat This is a _ _ _	**cat** This is a _ _ _	**bag** This is a _ _ _
pan This is a _ _ _	**rat** This is a _ _ _	**map** This is a _ _ _

Can you think of any words that rhyme with the words above?

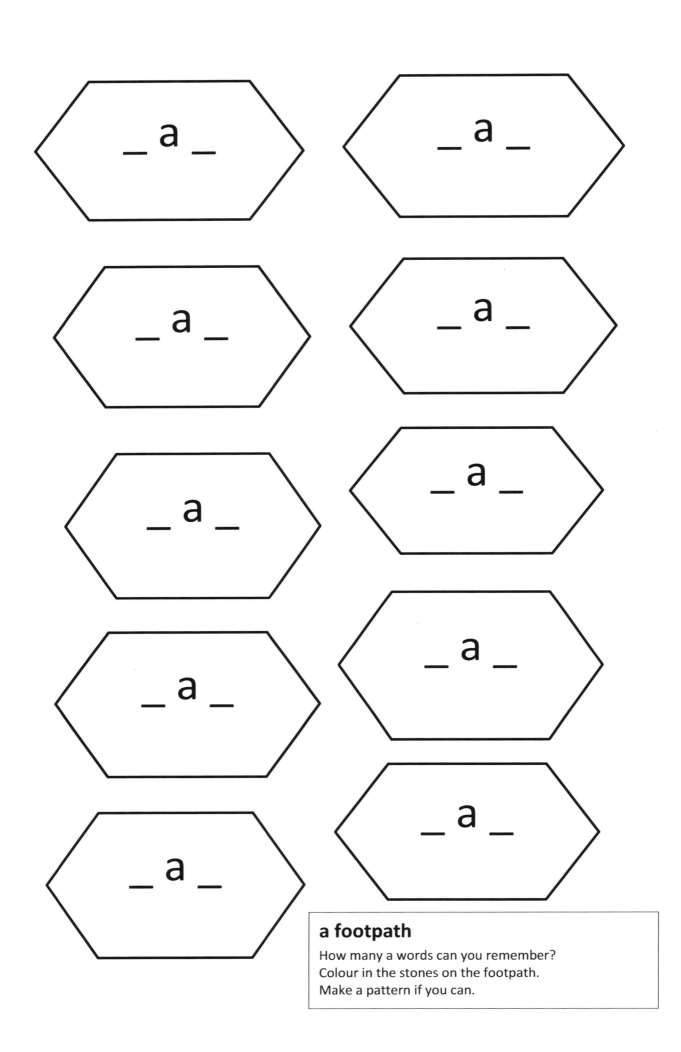

_ a _

_ a _

_ a _

_ a _

_ a _

_ a _

_ a _

_ a _

_ a _

a footpath

How many a words can you remember?
Colour in the stones on the footpath.
Make a pattern if you can.

mat	
tap	
fan	
man	
bag	

hat	
cat	
rat	
pan	
map	

Read each sentence, then and write the correct word in the gap below.

1. My dad is a _ _ _.

2. Water comes from a _ _ _.

3. In Geography we read a _ _ _.

4. My books are in my _ _ _.

5. Mum cooks dinner in a _ _ _.

6. A _ _ _ keeps you cool.

7. "Meow," said the _ _ _.

8. You wear a _ _ _ on your head.

9. Wipe your feet on the _ _ _.

Now make up a sentence yourself, using these words

hat   bat   rat

ă Dictation Sentences

1. The <u>man</u> has a <u>map</u>.
2. The <u>cat</u> likes the <u>fan</u>.
3. I like that <u>hat</u> and <u>bag</u>.
4. The <u>pan</u> is by the <u>tap</u>.
5. There is a <u>rat</u> on the <u>mat</u>.

Instructions for dictation sentences

1. Read the sentence aloud to the learner(s)
2. Learner(s) repeat sentence back to you
3. Learner(s) write full sentence in their book
4. Continue until all 5 sentences complete
5. Learner finds and highlights all words containing target phoneme
6. Teacher marks learner out of 10

hen

pen

bed

net

leg

pet

men

peg

web

ten

Tracking

Find the hidden words below. Each word is written only once.

1. pet
2. men
3. peg
4. web
5. ten
6. hen
7. pen
8. bed
9. net
10. leg

1. l g h w o w s a c a s v f e f v b b s p e t

2. w d c a s c f v f s w e q m e n d w f c f v

3. s c a d f r v b v g h n g p e g g f v s z a

4. c z f v d b g d z v h n v z d f w e b v z d

5. f v z t e n c d a v f b s n h m j k k , j j k

6. v n c b x z v t t h p r w d q f g t n h e n

7. F G F B V Z C P E N V G B F V D C S Z C

8. v f V Z D B E D d f z v g b d h b f v d c Y

9. t z f v b g f d v d f z s z n e t x v b g v f

10. d z c \ s d f g b h n m k m j h n g c l e g

Write the missing words, then copy the sentence

This is a _ _ _

_____

This is _ _ _

_____

This is a _ _ _

_____

This is a _ _ _

_____

This is _ _ _

_____

This is a _ _ _

_____

This is a _ _ _

_____

This is a _ _ _

_____

This is a _ _

_____

This is a _ _ _

_____

Silly sentences

Read each sentence. Then replace the underlined word with a rhyming word that makes sense.

1. The <u>den </u>laid an egg.

2. I write with my<u> men.</u>

3. She has a <u>bet </u>cat.

4. The footballer hurt his<u> shed.</u>

5. I sleep in a <u>ted.</u>

6. The spider spun a <u>keg.</u>

7. The ball went in the <u>set.</u>

8. Mum will <u>beg</u> out the washing.

9. Next birthday my brother will be <u>Ben</u>

10. <u>Len </u>sometimes have beards.

Connect 3 Game. The first learner to get 3 counters in a row wins. The learner must read the word correctly to place a counter on it.

bed	Ben	**fed**	hen
bet	**keg**	jet	men
let	net	**peg**	pet
pen	red	**leg**	set
ten	GET	den	beg

ĕ Dictation Sentences

1. My <u>pen</u> is in the <u>bed.</u>
2. The <u>hen</u> is in the <u>web</u>.
3. <u>Ten men</u> played football.
4. My <u>pet</u> has a bad <u>leg</u>.
5. Mum put a <u>peg</u> on the <u>net</u>.

Instructions for dictation sentences

1. Read the sentence aloud to the learner(s)
2. Learner(s) repeat sentence back to you
3. Learner(s) write full sentence in their book
4. Continue until all 5 sentences complete
5. Learner finds and highlights all words containing target phoneme
6. Teacher marks learner out of 10

bin

pig

tin

pin

lid

| lip |
| sip |
| win |
| big |
| six |

ĭ word search

Find the 10 ĭ words in the word search below. Write each word beneath.

```
B  I  N  B  L
S  I  P  I  I
Q  L  I  G  D
T  I  N  H  W
G  P  I  G  I
H  S  I  X  N
```

1. _ i _   2. _ i _

3. _ i _   4. _ i _

5. _ i _   6. _ i _

7. _ i _   8. _ i _

9. _ i _   10. _ i _

Test Sheet

Fold your test sheet along the lines.
Write the word next to each picture, then check your spelling by unfolding the sheet.

Picture	Write word	Check correct spelling
		bin
		pig
		tin
		pin
		lid
		lip
		win
		big
		six

Cloze

Use the words from your word search to fill the gaps below.

1. Half of 12 is _ _ _.

2. My _ _ _ sister is much older than me.

3. I hope my class will _ _ _ sports day.

4. The lady _ _ _ s her tea.

5. Put your rubbish in the _ _ _!

6. The _ _ _ of my lunchbox is stuck.

7. Be careful when you open that _ _ _ of beans!

8. _ _ _ 's babies are called piglets.

9. You can pop that balloon with a _ _ _.

Cross the river

Who can cross the river first? Use a dice to see how many steps you can take. For each step you take you must read the word on the stone correctly.

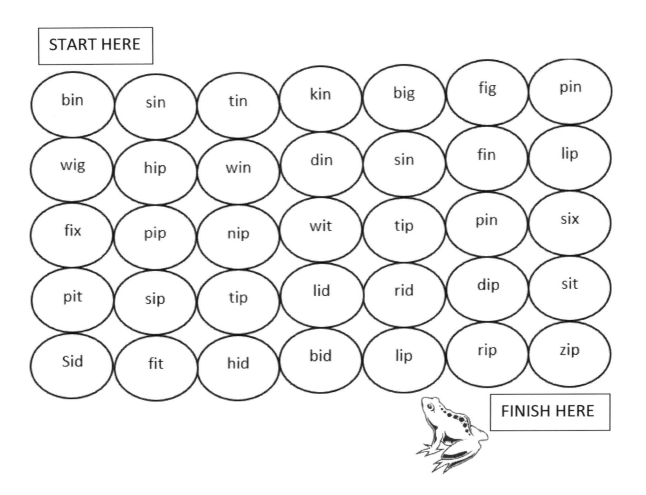

Note: This activity works best when enlarged to A3

ĭ Dictation Sentences

1. Put the <u>lid</u> on the <u>bin</u>.
2. Get the <u>pin</u> out the <u>tin</u>.
3. There are <u>six big pigs</u>.
4. Use your <u>lip</u> and <u>sip</u> the drink.
5. <u>Sid</u> said he will <u>win</u>.

Instructions for dictation sentences

1. Read the sentence aloud to the learner(s)
2. Learner(s) repeat sentence back to you
3. Learner(s) write full sentence in their book
4. Continue until all 5 sentences complete
5. Learner finds and highlights all words containing target phoneme
6. Teacher marks learner out of 10

hop

dot

dog

cot

top

mop

log

pot

fox

jog

Quiz

Guess the ten ŏ words then write them in the grid below

1. This is slower than a run.
2. This is a fast, sneaky wild animal that has cubs.
3. A houseplant lives in one of these.
4. A tree trunk after it has been chopped down.
5. You use this to wash the floor.
6. It's the opposite of bottom.
7. A baby sleeps in a _____.
8. It barks and whines and is Britain's favourite pet.
9. This is a spot, or a full stop.
10. Jumping on one leg.

1.		o	
2.		o	
3.		o	
4.		o	
5.		o	
6.		o	
7.		o	
8.		o	
9.		o	
10.		o	

You may want to cut these up to make a matching game

hop	
dot	.
dog	
cot	
top	

mop	
log	
pot	
fox	
jog	

Use the pictures from the matching game to spell ten ŏ words.

Cloze

Fit the correct ŏ word into the sentence below, so it makes sense.

1. To _ _ _ is to run slowly.

2. The tree has been chopped into _ _ _ s.

3. To _ _ _ is to run on one leg.

4. A _ _ _ is a fast, sneaky wild animal.

5. You clean the floor with a _ _ _.

6. _ _ _s and cats are both house pets.

7. Climb to the _ _ _ of the hill.

8. Put the plant into a _ _ _.

9. Put the baby into a _ _ _.

10.   A full stop is a _ _ _.

ŏ Dictation Sentences

1. <u>Jog</u> to the <u>top</u> of the hill.
2. Is that a <u>fox</u> or a <u>dog</u>?
3. The <u>cot</u> was made from a <u>log</u>.
4. You must <u>hop</u> on the <u>dot</u>.
5. Put the <u>mop</u> by the <u>pot</u>.

Instructions for dictation sentences

1. Read the sentence aloud to the learner(s)
2. Learner(s) repeat sentence back to you
3. Learner(s) write full sentence in their book
4. Continue until all 5 sentences complete
5. Learner finds and highlights all words containing target phoneme
6. Teacher marks learner out of 10

bus

sun

bun

jug

tug

fun
cut
run
gun
bug

Sorting exercise

Sort the words below into the 4 boxes.

bus	sun	bun	jug
fun	cut	run	gun
bug	tug	mug	rug

- **us**	- **un**
- **ug**	- **ut**

Extension

Can you think of any more ŭ words that would fit in? Add them to the boxes.

ŭ Crossword

Use the clues below to fill in the boxes.

1.		2.

Clues

Across

1. You catch these to travel by road.
2. A squirrel would eat this.
3. You shoot with this.

Down

1. A sweet cake.
2. Shines in the sky.
3. Pull hard in a _ _ _ of war.
4. Your pour a drink from this.

Name the picture

Circle the word that names the picture

sun tug cut	rug bus gun	bug jug mug
bug bus gun	rug run sun	bug run jug
run fun tug	bug run tug	cut jug bun
rug gun bug	cup rug tug	cup pup rug

Silly sentences

Read the caption. Draw the picture. Then write the caption underneath.

1. A jug on a bus	2. A cut in q gun	3. A bug having fun
4. A bun on a run	5. **A** bug tugs a rug	6. A mug in the sun

Silly sentences

1. A _ _ _ on a _ _ _.

2. A _ _ _ in a _ _ _.

3. A _ _ _ having _ _ _.

4. A _ _ _ on a _ _ _.

5. A bug _ _ _ s a _ _ _.

6. A _ _ _ in the _ _ _.

ŭ Dictation Sentences

1. I had a _bun_ and a _jug_ of tea.
2. _Tug_ on the door of the _bus._
3. The _bug_ is in the _sun._
4. _Run_ away if you see a _gun._
5. It's _fun_ to _cut_ buns.

Instructions for dictation sentences

1. Read the sentence aloud to the learner(s)
2. Learner(s) repeat sentence back to you
3. Learner(s) write full sentence in their book
4. Continue until all 5 sentences complete
5. Learner finds and highlights all words containing target phoneme
6. Teacher marks learner out of 10

st

stab

step

stamp

stem

stop

star

nest

start

stick

post

po_ _	
_ _ ick	
_ _ art	
ne _ _	
_ _ ar	
_ _ op	
st_ _	
_ _ amp	
_ _ ep	
_ _ ab	

Add "st" to each word.
What do you notice?

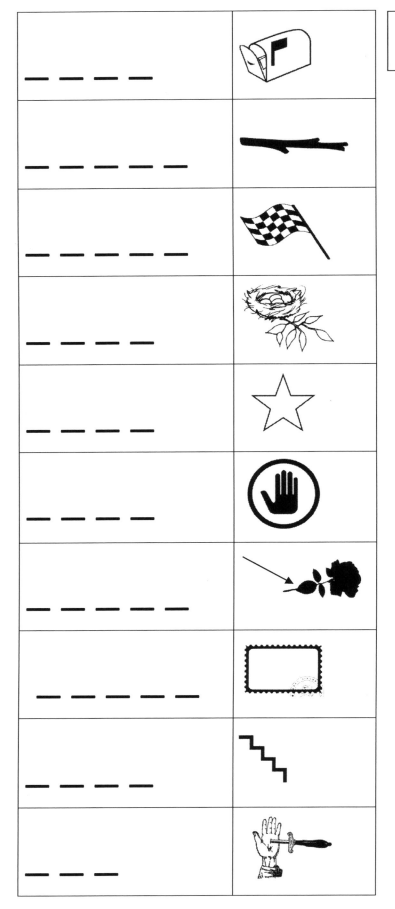

Connect 3 Game. The first learner to get 3 counters in a row wins. The learner must read the word correctly to place a counter on it.

stack	stir	**stork**	steer
stem	**just**	stamp	stuck
post	still	**stick**	step
stump	nest	**stab**	set
stay	STOP	start	*star*

Read this passage, then highlight all the words with the blend "st." *Remember that the blend "st" can be at the beginning or the end of a word.*

Birds

Birds must make nests from sticks. The best nest will last a long time. The best nest will still be there past winter time.

Baby birds are born in the nest, where they can rest and grow. Big mum birds can be nasty when they need food for their babies. With sharp claws they stab small animals. Then they fly fast to the nest.

When they grow up the babies learn to fly. Birds can fly fast. The best birds fly as far as the stars. They do not get lost.

Read each sentence, then and write the correct word in the gap below.

1. The murderer _ _ _ _s his victims.

2. The baby took his first _ _ _ _.

3. Put a _ _ _ _ _ on your letter.

4. Put your letter in the _ _ _ _ box.

5. The tall bit of a flower is the _ _ _ _.

6. A red light means you must _ _ _ _.

7. There is a _ _ _ _ in the night sky.

8. The birds have built a _ _ _ _.

9. _ _ _ _ _ means "begin".

10. Use glue to _ _ _ _ _ down the paper.

Now make up a sentence using these words:

stick   *nest*   *stem*

st Dictation Sentences

1. To <u>post</u> a card you must put a <u>stamp</u> on it.
2. The boy will <u>stab</u> his mate with a <u>stick.</u>
3. <u>Stop</u> and look at the <u>star.</u>
4. Take a <u>step</u> and <u>start</u> to walk.
5. You can <u>stick</u> the <u>stem</u> in your book.

Instructions for dictation sentences

7. Read the sentence aloud to the learner(s)
8. Learner(s) repeat sentence back to you
9. Learner(s) write full sentence in their book
10. Continue until all 5 sentences complete
11. Learner finds and highlights all words containing target phoneme
12. Teacher marks learner out of 10

snag

snow

snail

snap

snip

snug

snack

snort

sniff

snob

Name the picture

Circle the word that names the picture

snig snob snag	snow snag snop	snep snow snap
snail snob sney	snig snip snail	snop snug snag
snack snail snit	snutt snob snort	snob snort snick
snug snat sniff	snooze snick snob	snoy snoop snip

Extension

Can you circle all the made up words? There is one for each picture.

Quiz

Guess the ten sn words then write them in the grid below

1. You do this when you have a cold.
2. A person who thinks they are better than others.
3. A loud sniffing, grunting noise.
4. Something to eat on the run.
5. Warm and cosy.
6. You do this when you cut something
7. When something breaks into two.
8. A slimy small animal with a shell.
9. White stuff that falls in winter.
10. This is when something tears a little.

1.	s	n			
2.	s	n			
3.	s	n			
4.	s	n			
5.	s	n			
6.	s	n			
7.	s	n			
8.	s	n			
9.	s	n			
10.	s	n			

sn Bingo

- Make sure each learner has a bingo slip.
- Each learner should read the words on their slip out loud to check understanding.
- Teacher read out the list of words, making sure the learners check their bingo slips for each word as it is read.
- If the learner hears a word on their slip they should tick it off.
- The winner may get a line (horizontal, diagonal or vertical) or a full house.

sn bingo word list:

snip, snake, snag, snail, snow, snap, snooze, snoop, sniff, snack, snug, snort, snob

sniff	snack	snug
snoop	snip	snap
snob	snail	snake

sniff	snack	snooze
snake	snag	snap
snob	snail	snoop

sniff	snack	snort
snoop	snip	snap
snag	snug	snob

snip	snoop	snort
snow	snag	snap
snake	snooze	sniff

Climb the Ladder Game

Use a counter to mark your place on the ladder. Start at the bottom. Each time you are able to successfully complete the sentence you can climb a rung. If you can spell the word correctly you may climb another rung. The winner reaches the top first. It is possible to re-use sentences if you run out, but the learner *must spell a new word correctly* to climb a rung.

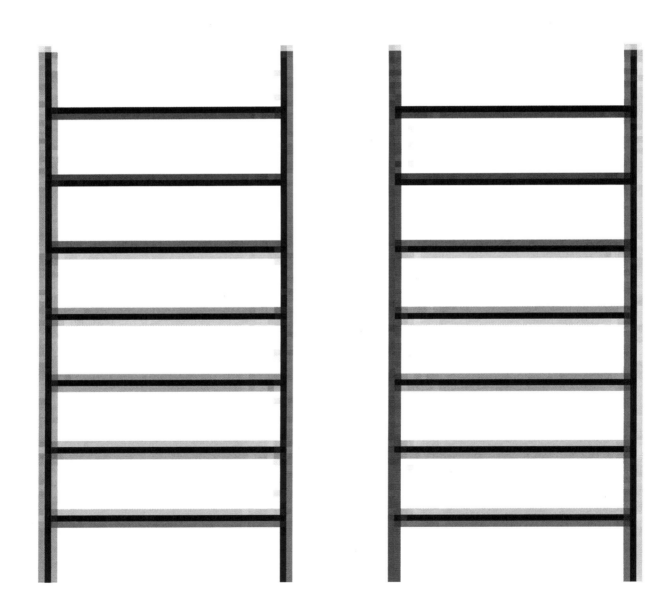

Climb the Ladder Game

Cut out each box into a strip. Place strips into a pile for use with the Climb the Ladder game.

I ripped my jeans on a nail and now I have a _ _ _ _.
I like it when it _ _ _ _ s a lot because it's white everywhere.
The _ _ _ _ _ came out because the garden was wet.
On holiday we had cards and we often played _ _ _ _.
When I have my hair cut sometimes they _ _ _ _ off too much.
In the winter it is nice to get _ _ _ _ in a warm bed.
At break I have a _ _ _ _ _.
A noise horses and pigs make is called a _ _ _ _ _.
My cold is making me _ _ _ _ _ _.
That lady thinks she is better than me, but she is just a _ _ _ _.
Careful! You will _ _ _ _ your pencil in half.

Snoopy, Snip and Pip

Snoopy is a dog. He lives in Scotland. Snoopy likes Scotland but he doesn't like the snow there. Snoopy has two mates, Pip and Snip. Snip is a snail. Pip is a snake. The pals play games. They like playing snooker and snap. Snoopy always wins at snooker. Snip always wins at snap. Pip never wins. Pip doesn't like games. Instead he likes to get snug. He has a snack and a snooze in bed.

sn Dictation Sentences

1. It is not good to _sniff_ and _snort._
2. That _snip_ made a _snag._
3. The _snail_ is _snug_ in his shell.
4. Tom will _snap_ his sled in the _snow._
5. The _snob_ is having a _snack._

Instructions for dictation sentences

1. Read the sentence aloud to the learner(s)
2. Learner(s) repeat sentence back to you
3. Learner(s) write full sentence in their book
4. Continue until all 5 sentences complete
5. Learner finds and highlights all words containing target phoneme
6. Teacher marks learner out of 10

spend

sport

spank

spy

speck

span

spot

spit

wasp

spin

_ _ in	
wa_ _	
_ _ y	
_ _ end	
_ _ ot	
_ _ it	
_ _ eck	.
_ _ ank	
_ _ ort	
_ _ ill	

Add "sp" to each word.
What do you notice?

		Now spell the other part of each word.
sp_ _		
_ _sp		
sp_		
sp_ _ _		
sp_ _		
sp_ _		
sp_ _ _		
sp_ _ _		
sp_ _ _		
sp_ _ _		

sp Crossword

Use the clues below to fill in the boxes.

Clues

Across

1. This might sting you.
2. This is another word for turning around fast.
3. Don't sp _ _ _ too much money!

Down

2. Very, very small
3. To hit something hard with your hand

Silly sentences

Read the caption. Draw the picture. Then write the caption underneath.

7. A wasp doing sport	8. A spill of spit	9. A spy being spanked
10. A spot spending money	11. The sport of spinning	12. A spill of drink

Silly sentences

1. A _ _ _ _ doing _ _ _ _ _.

2. A _ _ _ _ _ of _ _ _ _.

3. A _ _ _ being _ _ _ _ _ed.

4. A _ _ _ _ _ _ _ _ _ _ing money.

5. The _ _ _ _ _ _ of _ _ _ _ning.

6. A _ _ _ _ of drink.

sp Dictation Sentences

1. Look at that _speck_ of _spit._
2. Tom can _spin_ on the _spot._
3. Don't _spy_ on the _wasp._
4. You can _spend_ a lot on _sport._
5. If you _spill_ that you will get a _spank._

Instructions for dictation sentences

1. Read the sentence aloud to the learner(s)
2. Learner(s) repeat sentence back to you
3. Learner(s) write full sentence in their book
4. Continue until all 5 sentences complete
5. Learner finds and highlights all words containing target phoneme
6. Teacher marks learner out of 10

dr

drop

drag

drip

drug

drum

drink

dry

draw

drill

dress

Name the picture

Circle the word that names the picture

drip drink drep	dress dry drind	drah dry drug
dry dren drop	drum drink drun	draw drak drop
drill dress drit	drum drub drug	drap dry drag
drup drip dress	drain drum drob	drain drap drama

Extension

Can you circle all the made up words? There is one for each picture.

Quiz

Guess the ten dr words then write them in the grid below

1. A girl would wear this.
2. When something you hold falls down.
3. You do this with water, tea and coke.
4. You need this to make holes.
5. Used for making music.
6. An artist does this.
7. A tap can _ _ _ _ a little water.
8. To pull something along.
9. When the sun shines and it doesn't rain it is _ _ _.
10. A pill to make you feel better.

1.	d	r			
2.	d	r			
3.	d	r			
4.	d	r			
5.	d	r			
6.	d	r			
7.	d	r			
8.	d	r			
9.	d	r			
10.	d	r			

Climb the Ladder Game

Use a counter to mark your place on the ladder. Start at the bottom. Each time you are able to successfully complete the sentence you can climb a rung. If you can spell the word correctly you may climb another rung. The winner reaches the top first. It is possible to re-use sentences if you run out, but the learner *must spell a new word correctly* to climb a rung.

Climb the Ladder Game

Cut each box into a strip. Place strips into a pile for use with the Climb the Ladder game.

A desert is _ _ _.

You need to _ _ _ _ _ 8 glasses of water a day.

The builder is using a _ _ _ _ _.

The _ _ _ _ from the tap is annoying me!

It's the morning and you must get up and get _ _ _ _ _ed.

Don't _ _ _ _ that bag along the floor!

When we are ill sometimes we need _ _ _ _s to get better.

When you carry something you don't want to _ _ _ _ it.

_ _ _ _ me a nice picture!

In music lessons I like to play the _ _ _ _.

My best lesson at school is _ _ _ _ _.

Silly sentences

Read the caption. Draw the picture. Then write the caption underneath.

13.A girl drags a dress.	14.A drug on a drum.	15.A boy drawing a drip.
16.A man drops his drill.	17.A dry drink.	4. A drip plays the drum.

Silly sentences

1.A girl _ _ _ _ s a _ _ _ _ _ _.

2.A _ _ _ _ on a _ _ _ _.

3.A boy _ _ _ _ing a _ _ _ _ .

4.A man _ _ _ _s his _ _ _ _ _ _.

5.A _ _ _ _ _ _ _ _ _.

6. A _ _ _ _ plays the _ _ _ _.

Read this passage, then highlight all the words with the blend "dr"

Dr Drat and Dr Dregs

Dr Drat likes to drink tea with a drop of milk. She likes to eat dry cake. Sometimes Dr Drat drops her cake and drips tea on her dress. She makes a mess.

Dr Drat's work is drab. To help this she asked her boss, Dr Dregs, for a drawing to put on the wall and a drum to put in the corner. Dr Dregs made a drama. He asked Dr Drat to drop her plans and to drive home.

Now answer these questions

1. What does Dr Drat like to eat and drink at work?

_____

2. Why does she make a mess?

_____

3. How is Dr Drat's work?

_____

4. What did Dr Drat ask Dr Dregs for?

_____

5. Did she get what she wanted?

_____

dr Dictation Sentences

1. Bill is <u>dry</u> and needs a <u>drink.</u>
2. There is a <u>drip</u> on your <u>dress</u>.
3. If you <u>drag</u> the <u>drill</u> it will not work.
4. Tom will <u>draw</u> a <u>drum</u>.
5. Don't <u>drop</u> the <u>drug</u>.

Instructions for dictation sentences

1. Read the sentence aloud to the learner(s)
2. Learner(s) repeat sentence back to you
3. Learner(s) write full sentence in their book
4. Continue until all 5 sentences complete
5. Learner finds and highlights all words containing target phoneme
6. Teacher marks learner out of 10

trim

trip

tram

trot

trap

tramp
trunk
trust
trunk
truck

Tracking

tr words list

1. truck
2. trip
3. tram
4. trim
5. trust
6. tramp
7. trunk
8. trap
9. trot
10. try

Instructions

a) Track the tr words
b) Cross out the tr words
c) Do the sentences make sense now?

1. Stan try draws trap on trip his trim pad

2. tramp Tim sits trunk on tram the tap

3. trim Snip trot tram is a truck snail try

4. trust Slick try is sly as a tram trim fox

5. truck a tram kind man trot is trim sad

6. try Dr tramp Drat trim drops try tea try

tr Crossword

Use the clues below to fill in the boxes.

Clues

Across

1. Someone without a home.
2. Bigger than a car.

Down

1. You pack your stuff in this.
2. Runs like a train but needs no tracks.
3. To make an effort

Extension

Make a list of the tr words on this page. Can you spot all 6?

Silly sentences

Read each sentence. Then replace the underlined word with a rhyming word that makes sense.

1. Take care or you will pip!

2. I must fly harder to be nice.

3. Horses shot before they run.

4. The lamp has no home.

5. The ham is late.

6. I packed my things in a junk.

7. Don't ever bust a stranger.

8. My hair needs a skim.

9. The child played with his duck.

10.   I will open the slap door.

Connect 3 Game. The first learner to get 3 counters in a row wins. The learner must read the word correctly to place a counter on it.

try	trap	**trunk**	treat
trip	**trail**	train	troll
tray	try	**trust**	tree
trod	trim	**trap**	tramp
Tracy	TRACK	truck	*trot*

Read the text below

Tracy's **holiday**

Tracy is fed up. She lives in the town but does not like the trams, the tramps, and the trucks there. Tracy has packed a trunk and is taking a train to the country. As the train goes down the tracks Tracy can see the trees and the sky. She will ride on a pony and trot down a trail on it. Tracy will walk next to the trees and she will tread and trip in the mud. What a treat!

tr Dictation Sentences

1. I must <u>try</u> to <u>trust</u> her<u>.</u>
2. <u>Trams</u> and <u>trucks</u> can be toys.
3. Don't <u>trip</u> when you <u>trot</u>.
4. The <u>tramp</u> has a <u>trunk</u> with him.
5. I will go for my <u>trim</u> by <u>tram</u>.

Instructions for dictation sentences

1. Read the sentence aloud to the learner(s)
2. Learner(s) repeat sentence back to you
3. Learner(s) write full sentence in their book
4. Continue until all 5 sentences complete
5. Learner finds and highlights all words containing target phoneme
6. Teacher marks learner out of 10

crisp

crash

crib

cram

crop

crust

cross

crack

crab

cry

crisp	
cry	
crash	
crib	
crack	

cram	
crop	
cross	
crust	
crab	

cr wordsearch

Find the 10 words with the blend cr in the wordsearch below. Write each word beneath.

```
C   R   I   B   C   C
R   C   C   C   R   R
A   R   R   R   A   U
M   O   A   I   C   S
P   P   B   S   K   T
C   R   Y   P   B   T
S   C   R   O   S   S
C   R   A   S   H   C
```

1. C R _ _ _   2. C R _ _

3. C R _ _ _   4. C R _ _ _

5. C R _   6. C R _ _

7. C R _ _ _   8. C R _ _

9. C R _ _ _   10. C R _ _ _

cr Cloze Exercise

Use the words from your word search to fill the gaps below.

1. The baby is asleep in its _ _ _ _.

2. My snack today is _ _ _ _ _s.

3. Sad people sometimes _ _ _.

4. The driver _ _ _ _ _ed his car.

5. Don't _ _ _ _ too much stuff into that bag!

6. Too much rain is bad for the farmer's _ _ _ _s.

7. The hard bit of bread is called the _ _ _ _ _ _.

8. _ _ _ _ _ is another word for angry.

9. I dropped the cup and now it is _ _ _ _ _ _ed.

10. At the sea I saw a _ _ _ _ on a rock.

The crab

The crab lives in a crag in the rocks. His home is a small crack, where he can creep out into the sun when he wants to. The crab dislikes crowds. He likes the crash of the sea and the cry of a sea bird.

Write a sentence below about the crab

_____

_____

The crow

The crow likes the sky. He likes to fly in the sky. The crow likes to find food to eat. He will fly far to eat a crop. Or he will fly to town to find crumbs, crusts and crisps.

Write a sentence below about the crow

_____

_____

cr Dictation Sentences

1. Don't <u>cram</u> the car or you will <u>crash</u> it.
2. There was a <u>cry</u> from the <u>crib</u>.
3. I will eat a <u>crust</u> and some <u>crisps</u>.
4. Look at the <u>crab</u> in the <u>crack</u>.
5. The bad <u>crop</u> made the man <u>cross</u>

Instructions for dictation sentences

1. Read the sentence aloud to the learner(s)
2. Learner(s) repeat sentence back to you
3. Learner(s) write full sentence in their book
4. Continue until all 5 sentences complete
5. Learner finds and highlights all words containing target phoneme
6. Teacher marks learner out of 10

prom

pram

pray

prim

prop

prick

print

prod

prank

press

Match the pr word to the picture

prod   **pr**om   **pr**im   **pr**am

pray   **pr**ops   **pr**ick   **pr**int

      print   **pr**ank   **pr**ess

Test Sheet

Fold your test sheet along the lines.
Write the word next to each picture, then check your spelling by unfolding the sheet.

Picture	Write word	Check correct spelling
		press
		prim
		prick
		print
		prop
		prod
		pram
		pray
		prank
		prom

pr Bingo

- Make sure each learner has a bingo slip.
- Each learner should read the words on their slip out loud to check understanding.
- Teacher read out the list of words, making sure the learners check their bingo slips for each word as it is read.
- If the learner hears a word on their slip they should tick it off.
- The winner may get a line (horizontal, diagonal or vertical) or a full house.

pr bingo word list: prom, pram, pray, prim, prick, prop, print, prod, prank, press

prim	prank	pray
prom	press	print
press	prop	pram

prank	press	pray
prom	prod	print
prick	prop	pram

prom	prop	print
prom	prod	print
prim	prop	pram

pray	pram	print
prom	prod	press
prick	prom	prank

pr Cloze Exercise

Choose words from below to fill the gaps

1. A _ _ _ _ is like a party.

2. Get in the lift and _ _ _ _ _ the button.

3. In drama we use _ _ _ _s.

4. A pin could _ _ _ _ _ my skin.

5. The baby was in its _ _ _ _.

6. I _ _ _ _ in church.

7. The girl looked _ _ _ _ in her dress.

8. Please _ _ _ _ _ _ your work after you finish it.

9. A word for joke is _ _ _ _ _.

10. I will _ _ _ _ the sleeping man.

prince	prim	prom
prod	press	prick
pray	prop	print
pram	prank	present

Read the text below and highlight the pr words.

The Prince

It was printed in the press that the people wanted a prince. When the prince was born the people were happy. He had a gold pram and lots of presents.

When the prince grew up was lazy, played pranks and did not impress. His parents prayed that he would improve before he became king. They tried to protect the prince but people did not like him. They did not want him to be king.

The prince was sent away to learn to be nice, and that he could not have everything he preferred. He improved and became a nicer person. In the end the prince was a good king.

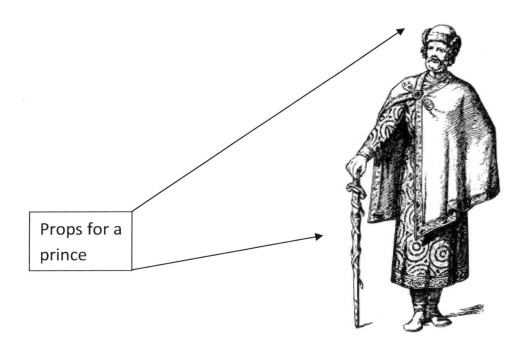

Props for a prince

pr Dictation Sentences

1. <u>Print</u> the list for the <u>prom</u>.
2. I will not <u>press</u> on the <u>pram</u>.
3. You can <u>prod</u> and <u>prick</u> the map.
4. The <u>prim</u> man will <u>pray</u>.
5. I need a <u>prop</u> for a <u>prank</u>.

Instructions for dictation sentences

1. Read the sentence aloud to the learner(s)
2. Learner(s) repeat sentence back to you
3. Learner(s) write full sentence in their book
4. Continue until all 5 sentences complete
5. Learner finds and highlights all words containing target phoneme
6. Teacher marks learner out of 10

grim

grip

gram

grab

grit

grand

grunt

grasp

grin

grid

		Add "gr" to each word.
_ _ id		
_ _ asp		
_ _ im		
_ _ am		
_ _ and		
_ _ ip		
_ _ ab		
_ _ it		
_ _ unt		

gr_ _	
gr_ _ _	
gr_ _	
gr_ _	
gr_ _ _	
gr_ _	
gr_ _	
gr_ _	
gr_ _ _	

Now complete each word.

Cross the river

Who can cross the river first? Use a dice to see how many steps you can take. For each step you take you must read the word on the stone correctly.

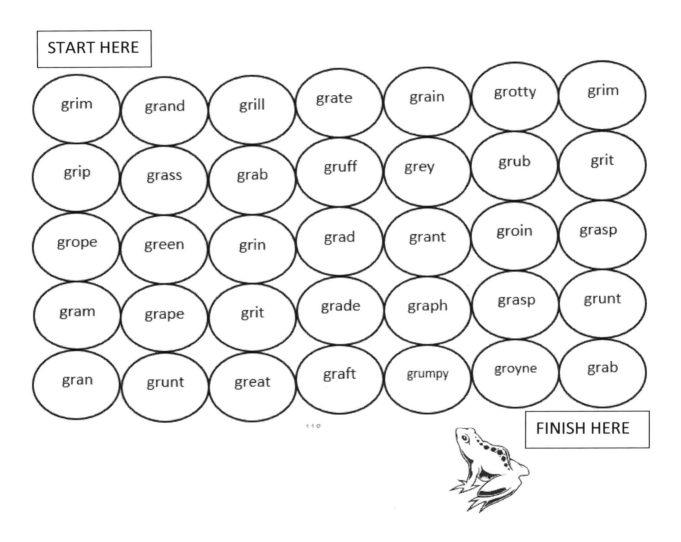

START HERE

grim	grand	grill	grate	grain	grotty	grim
grip	grass	grab	gruff	grey	grub	grit
grope	green	grin	grad	grant	groin	grasp
gram	grape	grit	grade	graph	grasp	grunt
gran	grunt	great	graft	grumpy	groyne	grab

FINISH HERE

Note: This activity works best when enlarged to A3

Cut and stick to match the beginnings of each sentence with the correct ending

It was a sad day so	**grip** onto trees.
In science we wrote our results	into the **grid**.
A **gram** is	**grit** onto the road.
The hotel by the sea	I will **grab** my coat
The baby **grasp**ed	less than a kilogram.
The pig made	his mum's hand.
Before I go out	is very **grand**.
Monkeys	had a big grin on his face.
The men were putting	everyone looked **grim**.
The man who won	a **grunting** noise

Now write the missing word in each sentence.

It was a sad day, so everyone looked _ _ _ _.

In Science we wrote our results into the _ _ _ _.

A _ _ _ _ is less than a kilogram.

The hotel by the sea is very _ _ _ _ _ _.

The baby _ _ _ _ _ed his mum's hand

The pig made a _ _ _ _ _ing sound.

Before I go out I will _ _ _ _ my coat

Monkeys _ _ _ _ onto trees.

The men were putting _ _ _ _ onto the road.

The man who won had a big _ _ _ _ on his face.

Read the passage below and highlight the words starting with gr

Gran and Gramps

Gran has grey hair. She always has a grin on her face.
I like gran because she makes tea and grills toast for me. Gran cheers me up when I feel grotty. She is a great friend.

Gramps is not like Gran. He is gruff and grumpy. He likes to watch TV. He grunts at the TV and grips the remote control in his hand. Gramps only likes the garden. He keeps the grass green, so it looks grand.

Below write two facts about Gran and Gramps

Gran

1._____

2._____

Gramps

1._____

2. _____

gr Dictation Sentences

1. We play a <u>grab</u> game in the <u>grid.</u>
2. That <u>grunt</u> made me <u>grin</u>.
3. Tom will <u>grasp</u> and <u>grip</u> your hand.
4. We have a <u>gram</u> of <u>grit</u>.
5. The <u>grim</u> man likes <u>grand</u> things.

Instructions for dictation sentences

1. Read the sentence aloud to the learner(s)
2. Learner(s) repeat sentence back to you
3. Learner(s) write full sentence in their book
4. Continue until all 5 sentences complete
5. Learner finds and highlights all words containing target phoneme
6. Teacher marks learner out of 10

gl

glad

glum

glee

glow

glint

gland

glass

glove

Draw a line to match the gl word to the picture.

glove   **gl**um   **gl**ee

glass   **gl**int   **gl**ad

gland   **gl**ow

Quiz

Guess the 8 gl words then write them in the grid below

1. A torch does this in the dark
2. I am _ _ _ _ I finished the test.
3. To shine a little bit.
4. Feeling really happy.
5. Feeling a bit sad.
6. You drink from this,
7. This is a part of the body.
8. You put this on your hand.

1.	g	l			
2.	g	l			
3.	g	l			
4.	g	l			
5.	g	l			
6.	g	l			
7.	g	l			
8.	g	l			

Noughts and Crosses

Make sure you read the word underneath
before you draw your nought or cross.

glee	glint	glove
glow	glum	glass
gloom	gland	glad

Silly sentences

Read the caption. Draw the picture. Then write the caption underneath.

1. A glad glove	2. A glum glass.
3. A gleeful gland	4. A glint in the gloom.

Silly sentences

1. A _ _ _ _ _ _ _ _ _.

2. A _ _ _ _ _ _ _ _ _.

3. A _ _ _ _ful _ _ _ _ _

4. A _ _ _ _ _ in the _ _ _ _ _.

gl Dictation Sentences

1. I am <u>glad</u> I have my <u>glove</u> on.
2. Try to be <u>glad</u> and not <u>glum</u>.
3. The <u>glow</u> is from over there.
4. My <u>gland</u> hurts.
5. That <u>glint</u> is from the <u>glass.</u>

Instructions for dictation sentences

1. Read the sentence aloud to the learner(s)
2. Learner(s) repeat sentence back to you
3. Learner(s) write full sentence in their book
4. Continue until all 5 sentences complete
5. Learner finds and highlights all words containing target phoneme
6. Teacher marks learner out of 10

clip

clap

club

clam

claw

clump

click

climb

clock

clash

Name the picture

Circle the word that names the picture.

climb clyhn clips		click clip clinz		clap clim clump	
clav clip climb		clever clump cli		clash clamp clor	
clump clamp clat		clum clock clash		club claw cleg	
clip clat clay		clam clup clap		clid claws clama	

Extension

Can you circle all the made up words? There is one for each picture.

132

cl words

Write the words into the correct shaped box

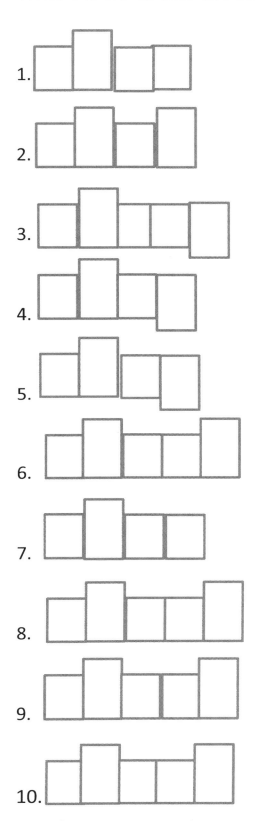

1.

2.

3.

4.

5.

6.

7.

8.

9.

10.

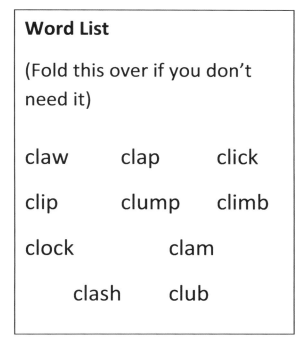

Word List

(Fold this over if you don't need it)

claw   clap   click

clip   clump   climb

clock   clam

          clash   club

cl Bingo

- Make sure each learner has a bingo slip.
- Each learner should read the words on their slip out loud to check understanding.
- Teacher read out the list of words, making sure the learners check their bingo slips for each word as it is read.
- If the learner hears a word on their slip they should tick it off.
- The winner may get a line (horizontal, diagonal or vertical) or a full house.

Bingo word list:

clock, click, clip, clap, clump, climb, clam, clash, club, claw

clock	click	clam	claw
clip	clap	club	club
clump	climb	clash	clip

click	clam	clump	club
claw	club	clash	clock
clock	clock	climb	clap

clash	clip	clap	club
clam	clump	climb	clip
clock	clap	claw	click

click	claw	clump	clump
club	club	clash	clock
clap	clock	climb	clap

Silly sentences

Read each sentence. Then replace the underlined word with a rhyming word that makes sense. The word will start with cl.

1. Don't trip on that <u>dump</u> of grass!

2. She has a nice <u>pip</u> in her hair.

3. <u>Slap</u> along to the beat.

4. It was a <u>slime</u> up to the top of the hill.

5. The <u>smock</u> made a ticking sound.

6. A <u>ham</u> is a shell fish.

7. The cat has hurt its <u>saw</u>.

8. Come and join in the chess <u>blub</u>.

9. That bell makes a <u>flash</u>ing sound.

10. When you put your seat belt on you will hear a <u>tick</u>.

blow

blob

blunt

blank

blush

blast

blink

black

block

blind

_ _ ack	
_ _ ob	
_ _ ind	
_ _ ow	
_ _ ast	
_ _ ock	
_ _ ink	
_ _ ush	
_ _ ank	
_ _ unt	

Add "bl" to each word.

bl _ _ _		Add the ending to each "bl" word.
bl _ _		
bl _ _ _		
bl _ _		
bl _ _ _		
bl _ _ _		
bl _ _ _		
bl _ _ _		
bl _ _ _		
bl _ _ _		

139

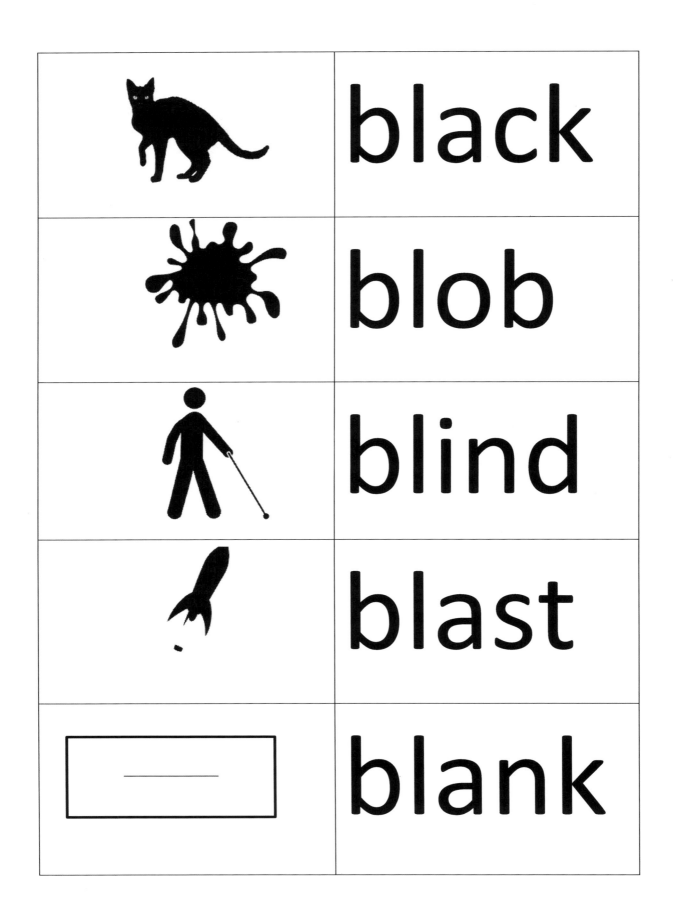

	black
	blob
	blind
	blast
	blank

	blush
	block
	blow
	blink
	blunt

bl sentences

Use the picture clues to complete the sentences below.

1. The _ _ _ _ _ cat will drink the milk.

2. Clean that _ _ _ _ off your top!

3. That old man with a stick is _ _ _ _ _ _.

4. _ _ _ _ _ your nose!

5. _ _ _ _ _ _ means "not sharp."

6. Soon the rocket will _ _ _ _ _ off.

7. Tim plays with his _ _ _ _ _s.

8. The sun makes me _ _ _ _ _ _.

9. When I feel hot I _ _ _ _ _ _.

10. Fill in the _ _ _ _ _s.

Read the story below and highlight the bl words

Bill, Sam, Blobs and Blocks

Bill loved his blocks. They were blue, green and black. Bill liked to sit and bang on the floor with them. One day he was doing this when his brother Sam was having porridge. Sam didn't like it. It was bland. Sam chucked it on the floor. A big blob hit Bill on his eye. Bill blinked but could not see. He was blind. Everything was a blur. His head was blank. Bill stood up. He hit his head on the table and fell down. There was a bit of blood. "Oh bless," said Mum, as she blotted his bleeding head. Sam blushed. He had not wanted to hurt Bill. He was in for it now!

Now answer these questions

1. Why does Bill love his blocks?

   _____

2. What did Sam do with his porridge?

   _____

3. What went into Bill's eye?

   _____

4. What did Mum say?

   _____

5. Why did Sam blush?

   _____

Extension

Write the next sentence in the story. What happens to Sam?

bl Dictation Sentences

1. The <u>blast</u> made us <u>blink</u>.
2. A <u>blind</u> man can just see <u>black</u>.
3. The <u>blocks</u> are <u>blunt</u>.
4. I <u>blush</u> when I go <u>blank</u>.
5. You must not <u>blow</u> on the <u>blob</u>.

Instructions for dictation sentences

1. Read the sentence aloud to the learner(s)
2. Learner(s) repeat sentence back to you
3. Learner(s) write full sentence in their book
4. Continue until all 5 sentences complete
5. Learner finds and highlights all words containing target phoneme
6. Teacher marks learner out of 10

flip

flap

flan

flat

flag

flow
fly
fling
flash
flock

fl word search

Find the 10 words with the blend fl in the word search below. Write each word beneath.

```
F   L   A   S   H   Y
L   F   L   I   P   F
A   H   F   L   A   P
G   F   L   A   T   F
P   A   Y   F   L   L
Y   F   L   A   N   O
F   L   I   N   G   W
F   L   O   C   K   K
```

1. F L _ _

2. F L _ _

3. F L _ _ _

4. F L _ _

5. F L _ _ _

6. F L _ _

7. F L _ _ _

8. F L _

9. F L _ _

10. F L _ _

fl Cloze Exercise

Use the words from your word search to fill the gaps below.

1. The English _ _ _ _ is red and white.

2. A _ _ _ _ is smaller than a house.

3. Mum made a _ _ _ _ for tea.

4. A _ _ _ bit me.

5. A _ _ _ _ _ of birds is in the sky.

6. There was a _ _ _ _ _ and a puff of smoke.

7. _ _ _ _ _ means throw.

8. Careful when you _ _ _ _ the pancake.

9. The bird _ _ _ _ s its wings.

10. Water _ _ _ _ s from the tap.

Test Sheet

Fold your test sheet along the lines.
Write the word next to each picture, then check your spelling by unfolding the sheet.

Picture	Write word	Check correct spelling
		flag
		flip
		flat
		flan
		flap
		fly
		fling
		flock
		flash
		flow

Connect 3 Game. The first learner to get 3 counters in a row wins. The learner must read the word correctly to place a counter on it.

fly	flat	**flee**	fleet
flop	**float**	fluff	flick
flea	fleet	**flag**	flame
flan	flock	**flash**	flip
flit	FLOW	flower	*flake*

Read the text below and highlight the fl words.

Then write them into the boxes below.

What am I?

I can flap my wings and fly.

I flick my wand.

I do not flop because I am light.

I have flowing hair.

I come with a flash and a puff of smoke.

1.	f	l			
2.	f	l			
3.	f	l			
4.	f	l			
5.	f	l			
6.	f	l			
7.	f	l			

Extension

Can you guess who is being described?

fl Dictation Sentences

1. The <u>flag</u> <u>flaps</u> in the wind.
2. <u>Fling</u> the bad <u>flan</u> into the bin.
3. <u>Club</u> members do not <u>clash</u>.
4. The wet fish <u>flip</u> and <u>flash</u>.
5. A <u>flock</u> of birds <u>fly</u> past.

Instructions for dictation sentences

1. Read the sentence aloud to the learner(s)
2. Learner(s) repeat sentence back to you
3. Learner(s) write full sentence in their book
4. Continue until all 5 sentences complete
5. Learner finds and highlights all words containing target phoneme
6. Teacher marks learner out of 10

plan

plug

plod

plum

play

plump
play
plus
pluck
plane

Tracking

Find the hidden words below. Each word is written only once.

1. plan
2. plum
3. plod
4. plus
5. plug
6. play
7. plump
8. pluck
9. plant
10. plane

1.   lghswowsacaplansvfefvb

2.   wdcascfvfswezplumfvgdw

3.   srvbvghngpeggfvszaplode

4.   cplusmzfvdbsnvzdfwebvzd

5.   fvztencdplugavfbeenk,jjk

6.   vncbxzvtthprwdqfgplayhe

7.   dzc\plumpkmjhngclegfleg

8.   FGFGBFVDpluckFGJKLCSZC

9.   fVZDBEDffvdcplantHFYH

10.   planegthfdvdfzsznetxvbg

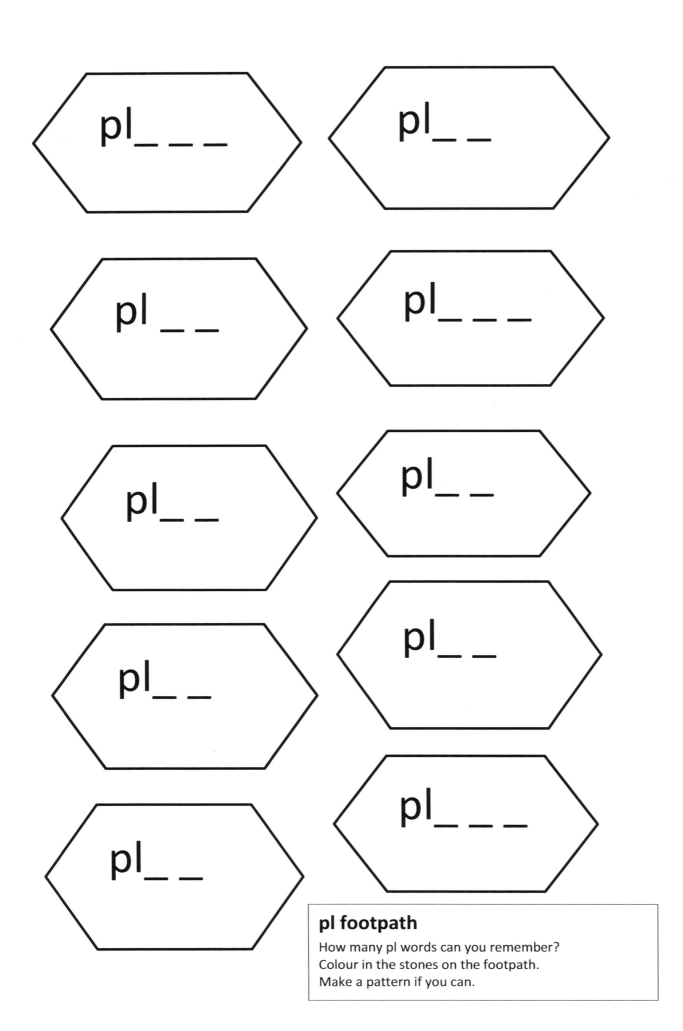

pl _ _ _

pl _ _

pl _ _

pl _ _ _

pl _ _

pl _ _

pl _ _

pl _ _

pl _ _

pl _ _ _

pl footpath

How many pl words can you remember?
Colour in the stones on the footpath.
Make a pattern if you can.

pl Cloze Exercise

Choose words from below to fill the gaps.

1. Add is another word for _ _ _ _.

2. A _ _ _ _ is a juicy fruit.

3. I went on holiday on a _ _ _ _ _.

4. I _ _ _ _ to work hard this year.

5. The _ _ _ _ _ grew from a seed.

6. You need to _ _ _ _ in your computer.

7. To walk slowly is to _ _ _ _.

8. You can _ _ _ _ _ a flower from the garden.

9. Sam will _ _ _ _ after he has cleaned his room.

10.   That plum looks _ _ _ _ _ and ripe.

plump	play	pluck
plod	plug	plant
plan	plane	plus
	plum	

Cross the river

Who can cross the river first? Use a dice to see how many steps you can take. For each step you take you must read the word on the stone correctly.

Extension: Colour code the blends pl and spl. Spot the odd one out!

START HERE

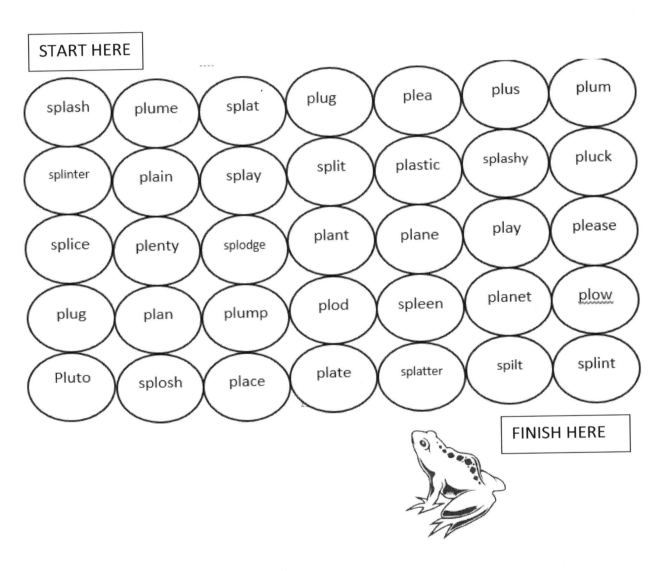

| splash | plume | splat | plug | plea | plus | plum |

| splinter | plain | splay | split | plastic | splashy | pluck |

| splice | plenty | splodge | plant | plane | play | please |

| plug | plan | plump | plod | spleen | planet | plow |

| Pluto | splosh | place | plate | splatter | spilt | splint |

FINISH HERE

Note: This activity works best when enlarged to A3

158

Read the text below highlight the fl words.

Would you like to be a farmer?

Farming in Kent

Farmers in Kent rear lambs and grow apples and plums. Working on a farm is hard, plain work. There is plenty to do, and not much time for play. Here is a plan of what farmers do during the year.

Autumn

Plough and plant crops.

Winter

Care for animals.

Spring

Make sure lambs are plump.

Summer

Pluck plums and apples.

pl Dictation Sentences

1. One <u>plus</u> one is two.
2. Tell her not to <u>play</u> with the <u>plug</u>.
3. Later I <u>plan</u> to <u>play</u> cards.
4. I will <u>pluck</u> a <u>plum</u> from the <u>plant</u>.
5. The <u>plump</u> man will <u>plod</u> home.

Instructions for dictation sentences

1. Read the sentence aloud to the learner(s)
2. Learner(s) repeat sentence back to you
3. Learner(s) write full sentence in their book
4. Continue until all 5 sentences complete
5. Learner finds and highlights all words containing target phoneme
6. Teacher marks learner out of 10

nk

bank

link

drink

sink

thank

chunk

pink

think

stink

wink

nk words

Write the words into the correct shaped box.
What do you notice about the end shape of each word?

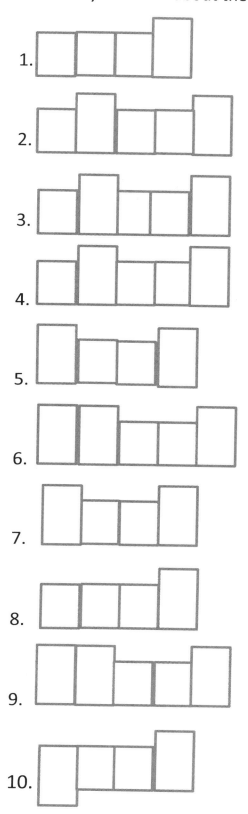

1.

2.

3.

4.

5.

6.

7.

8.

9.

10.

Word List

wink   stink

pink

think   chunk

sink

thank   drink

link   bank

nk Crossword

Use the clues below to fill in the boxes.

Clues

Across

1. Pieces or parts of something bigger.
2. What you do with milk
3. In a pen.
4. A colour.

Down

1. Used for skating.
2. Part of a chain.
3. Used for washing.

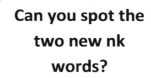

Can you spot the
two new nk
words?

1. _ _ _

2. _ _ _ _

bank	
link	
drink	
sink	
thank	

chunks	
pink	
think	
stink	
wink	

Cut and stick to match the beginnings of each sentence with the correct ending.

I've got no money	in the **sink.**
I **think** that	feel sick.
After my run	I will want a **drink.**
I want to buy	on the web.
Give me a chunk	in the **bank.**
We said thank you	I need a rest.
My pal gave me	the **pink** dress.
Put the dish	a **wink** and a smile.
The **stink** made us	for the gift.
There is a **link**	of your bar.

Read the text below highlight the nk words.

A bad day for Frank

Frank had no water at home. A man came to fix the sink and the water tank. Frank had no cash, so he had to run to the bank. When Frank got back he ran to the sink. He was hot and pink, and needed a drink.

Frank drank some water and had some chunks of bread. "Wow," said Frank "I needed that! Now I will have a shower."

Now answer these questions

1. What did the man come to fix?

_____

2. Why did Frank run to the bank?

_____

3. What made Frank feel better?

_____

4. Why did Frank need a shower?

_____

nk Dictation Sentences

1. I will say <u>thank</u> you with a <u>wink.</u>
2. There is a <u>stink</u> from the <u>sink.</u>
3. I can't <u>think</u> of the web <u>link.</u>
4. Give me a <u>chunk</u> of the <u>pink</u> sweet.
5. I got a <u>drink</u> at the <u>bank.</u>

Instructions for dictation sentences

1. Read the sentence aloud to the learner(s)
2. Learner(s) repeat sentence back to you
3. Learner(s) write full sentence in their book
4. Continue until all 5 sentences complete
5. Learner finds and highlights all words containing target phoneme
6. Teacher marks learner out of 10

band

land

stand

and

pond

| mind |
| wand |
| hand |
| end |
| sand |

ba_ _		Add "nd" to each word.
la_ _		
sta_ _		
a_ _	**+**	
min_ _		
wa_ _		
ha_ _		
sa_ _		
e_ _		
po_ _		

_ _ nd		Add the beginning to each "nd" word.
_ _ nd		
_ _ _ nd		
_ nd	+	
_ _ _ nd		
_ _ nd		
_ _ nd		
_ _ nd		
_ nd		
_ _ nd		

Cross the river

Who can cross the river first? Use a dice to see how many steps you can take. For each step you take you must read the word on the stone correctly.

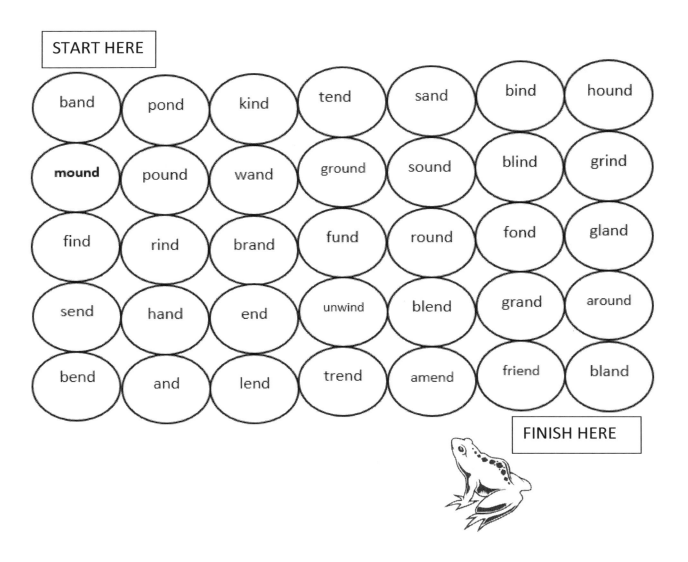

START HERE

band	pond	kind	tend	sand	bind	hound
mound	pound	wand	ground	sound	blind	grind
find	rind	brand	fund	round	fond	gland
send	hand	end	unwind	blend	grand	around
bend	and	lend	trend	amend	friend	bland

FINISH HERE

Note: This activity works best when enlarged to A3

174

Quiz

Guess the 10 nd words then write them in the grid below

1. Do you _ _ _ _ if I sit down here?
2. The _ _ _ _ are playing some good music.
3. You make magic with this.
4. This has 5 fingers.
5. The opposite of the start.
6. Fish swim in this.
7. This word joins two things together. Fish _ _ _ chips.
8. Lots of this yellow stuff at the seaside.
9. You keep your feet on this.
10. When boats and planes arrive.

				n	d
1.				n	d
2.				n	d
3.				n	d
4.				n	d
5.				n	d
6.				n	d
7.				n	d
8.				n	d
9.				n	d
10.				n	d

Silly sentences

Read each sentence. Then replace the underlined word with a rhyming word that makes sense. The word will end with nd

1. The ship is in sight of <u>hand</u>.

2. The fairy waved her magic <u>fond</u>.

3. It's time to <u>bland</u> up and go.

4. Plus means <u>grand</u>.

5. She waved her <u>land</u> at me.

6. The <u>mound</u> was wet under my feet.

7. I like <u>hand</u> on the beach.

8. She works as a child <u>find</u>er.

9. It was the <u>bend</u> of the day.

10.   That <u>gland</u> plays good music.

Read the text below highlight the nd words.

Miss Kind's New Year Resolutions.

1. Wipe sand and dirt from my shoes.

2. Mend the holes in my socks.

3. Tend to the garden more often.

4. Clean the pond more often.

5. Send birthday cards to family and friends

6. Find time to spend with family and friends.

7. Mind my sister's children to give her a rest.

8. Stand on the bus if others need my seat.

9. Relax and unwind on Saturdays.

10. Lend a hand at church on Sundays.

nd Dictation Sentences

1. Don't <u>stand</u> in the <u>pond</u>.
2. There was <u>sand</u> on the <u>ground</u>.
3. The <u>band</u> will <u>land</u> at six.
4. My <u>hand</u> and <u>foot</u> are bad.
5. Feel the <u>end</u> of the <u>wand</u>.

Instructions for dictation sentences

1. Read the sentence aloud to the learner(s)
2. Learner(s) repeat sentence back to you
3. Learner(s) write full sentence in their book
4. Continue until all 5 sentences complete
5. Learner finds and highlights all words containing target phoneme
6. Teacher marks learner out of 10

long

bang

sing

rung

song

lung
thing
cling
sling
spring

ng word search

Find the 10 words with the blend ng in the word search below. Write each word beneath.

```
S    P    R    I    N    G
L    F    S    O    N    G
I    H    I    L    R    T
N    F    N    U    R    T
G    A    G    N    U    H
B    A    N    G    N    I
C    L    I    N    G    N
F    L    L    O    N    G
```

1. _ _ N G   2. _ _ N G

3. _ _ _ _ N G   4. _ _ N G

5. _ _ _ N G   6. _ _ _ N G

7. _ _ _ N G   8. _ _ N G

9. _ _ N G   10. _ _ N G

lung

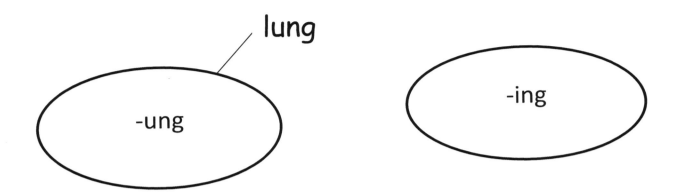

-ung

-ing

Use your wordsearch to write down words with these endings.

Can you think of more?

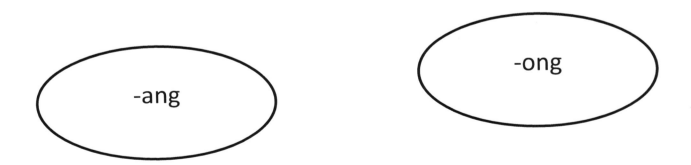

-ang

-ong

182

ng Cloze Exercise

Use the words from your word search to fill the gaps below.

1. In _ _ _ _ _ _ it gets warmer and greener.

2. My arm is broken and in a _ _ _ _ _.

3. Baby monkeys _ _ _ _ _ to their mums.

4. I had to go home as I forgot some_ _ _ _ _.

5. Jill can _ _ _ _ well.

6. The door shut with a _ _ _ _.

7. I won the _ _ _ _ jump on Sports Day.

8. Sing me a nice _ _ _ _.

9. We breathe with our _ _ _ _s.

10.   Careful! One _ _ _ _ of the ladder is

    broken.

Connect 3 Game. The first learner to get 3 counters in a row wins. The learner must read the word correctly to place a counter on it.

spring	bang	**sing**	ring
sting	**string**	swing	fang
rung	hang	**sling**	**prong**
song	wing	**belong**	cling
lung	BRING	thing	*king*

Read the text below highlight the ng words.

Dear Sir,

Please help!

I moved next door to you last spring. The noise from your flat is so bad that I can't stand it any longer.

I can hear all kinds of things from your flat. It's okay to sing a few songs, but you sing at the top of your lungs. And I hear loud bangs at all times of day and night.

Also, your kids swing and cling to the trees in the garden all day. I can't get any rest at all.

Yours sincerely

Tom Chang

Make a list of Tom Chang's complaints below

1. _____

2. _____

3. _____

ng Dictation Sentences

1. The birds start to _sing_ in _spring_.
2. I fell from the top _rung_ and hurt my _lung_.
3. That _thing_ is very _long._
4. The _song_ will stop with a _bang_.
5. It hurts if you _cling_ onto my _sling_.

Instructions for dictation sentences

1. Read the sentence aloud to the learner(s)
2. Learner(s) repeat sentence back to you
3. Learner(s) write full sentence in their book
4. Continue until all 5 sentences complete
5. Learner finds and highlights all words containing target phoneme
6. Teacher marks learner out of 10

ant

mint

bent

tent

hunt

front

point

plant

print

want

Name the picture

Circle the word that names the picture.

point pont plant	ent ant aunt	tent clent bent
want clent print	bant mint bent	bent sent pont
want sent wunt	print ront burnt	sont hunt stunt
tent mint fent	bent front slunt	sont hunt point

Extension

Can you circle all the made-up words? There is one for each picture.

Test Sheet

Fold your test sheet along the lines.
Write the word next to each picture, then check your spelling by unfolding the sheet.

Picture	Write word	Check correct spelling
		plant
		ant
		print
		want
		point
		bent
		hunt
		front
		mint

Climb the Ladder Game

Use a counter to mark your place on the ladder. Start at the bottom. Each time you are able to successfully complete the sentence you can climb a rung. If you can spell the word correctly you may climb another rung. The winner reaches the top first. It is possible to re-use sentences if you run out, but the learner *must spell a new word correctly* to climb a rung.

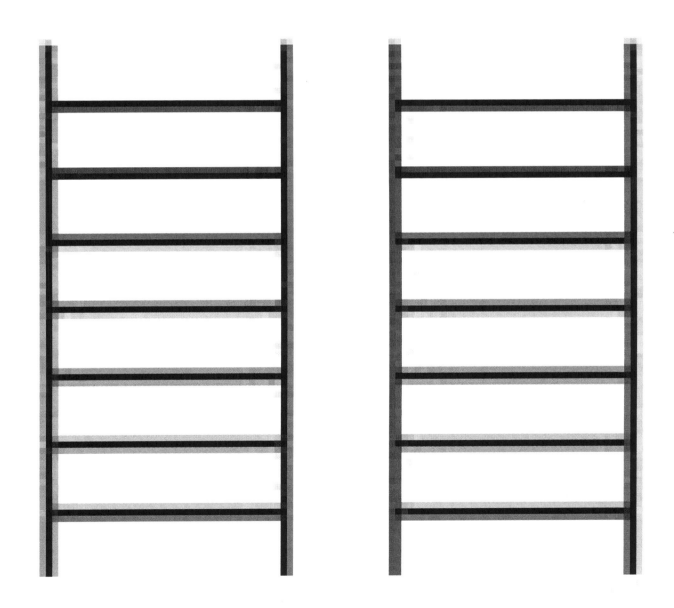

Climb the Ladder Game

Cut each box into a strip. Place each strip into a pile for use in the Climb the Ladder game

I am a small black animal. What am I?
You suck me to make your mouth smell nice. What am I?
I show you the way. What am I?
I am not straight. What am I?
I and green and I grow. What am I?
I am a feeling of needing something. What am I?
I am the opposite of back. What am I?
I am from a printer. What am I?
You use me when you are camping. What am I?
This word means to kill for sport or food. What is it?
I am sharp. What am I?

Silly sentences

Read the caption. Draw the picture. Then write the caption underneath.

1. A man pointing at a plant.	2. A tent with print on it.	3. An ant in front of the class.
4. A girl hunting for a mint.	5. The plant is bent over.	4. Aunt has sent me a letter.

Silly sentences

1. A man _ _ _ _ ing at a _ _ _ _ _.

2. A _ _ _ _ with _ _ _ _ on it.

3. An _ _ _ in _ _ _ _ of the class.

4. A girl _ _ _ _ing for a _ _ _ _.

5. The _ _ _ _ is _ _ _ _ over.

6. _ _ _ _ has _ _ _ _ me a letter.

Read the text below highlight the nt words.

Camping with Aunt

Last summer I was sent to my aunt and she took me camping. We spent a week living in a tent at Saint Mary's Bay. It was nice there. There were lots of plants in front of the tent. There were a few flies and ants, but the burnt smell from the campfire kept them away. Each night we sucked mints, chanted songs and had a great time. We will make a point of going back next year.

Now label the objects below

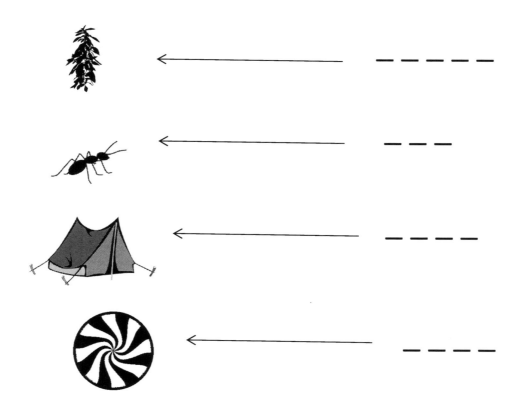

nt Dictation Sentences

1. I will <u>hunt</u> for my lost <u>mint</u>.
2. There is an <u>ant</u> in the <u>tent</u>.
3. I <u>want</u> to <u>print</u> it out.
4. The <u>plant</u> is <u>bent</u>.
5. <u>Point</u> at the <u>front</u> of it.

Instructions for dictation sentences

1. Read the sentence aloud to the learner(s)
2. Learner(s) repeat sentence back to you
3. Learner(s) write full sentence in their book
4. Continue until all 5 sentences complete
5. Learner finds and highlights all words containing target phoneme
6. Teacher marks learner out of 10

lamp

camp

ramp

bump

jump

plump

hump

lump

chimp

stamp

Tracking

Find the hidden words below. Each word is written only once.

1. lamp
2. lump
3. camp
4. stamp
5. chimp
6. jump
7. plump
8. hump
9. ramp
10. bump

1.   l g h s w o w s a c a l a m p s v f e f v b

2.   w d c a s c f v f s w e z l u m p f v g d w

3.   s r v b v g h n g p e g g f v s z a c a m p

4.   c m z f v d b s t a m p n v z d f w e b v z

5.   f v z t c h i m p e n c d a v f b e e n k , j

6.   v n c b x z v t t h p r j u m p w d q f g h

7.   d z c \ p l u m p k m j h n g c l e g f l e g

8.   F G F G B F V D F G J K L C S Z C h u m p

9.   f r a m p V Z D B E D d f f v d c H F Y H

10. g t h f d v d f b u m p z s z n e t x v b g

Extension

See if you can hide a "mp" word in some letters. Try below.

198

mp words

Write the words into the correct shaped box.
What do you notice about the end shape of each word?

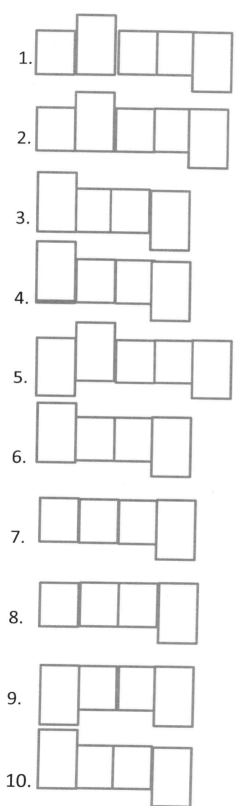

1.

2.

3.

4.

5.

6.

7.

8.

9.

10.

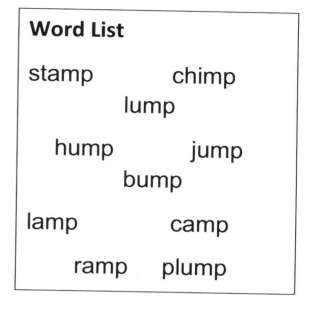

Word List

stamp   chimp
           lump

    hump   jump
           bump

lamp   camp

     ramp   plump

lamp	
camp	
ramp	
bump	
jump	

plump	
hump	
lump	
chimp	
stamp	

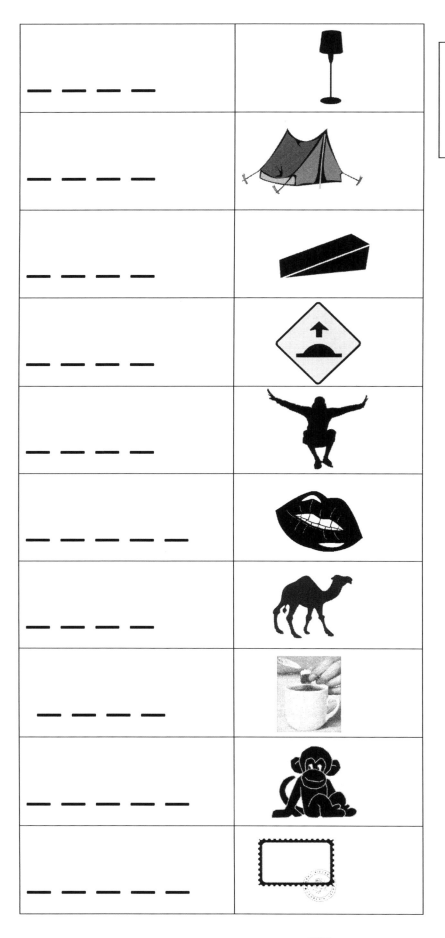

Can you spell the "mp" words from the matching game?

mp Cloze Exercise

Choose words from below to fill the gaps.

1. I have a _ _ _ _ by my bed.

2. In the summer hols we go _ _ _ _ing.

3. Do you want a _ _ _ _ of sugar?

4. Camels store water in their _ _ _ _ s.

5. Drive slowly on the _ _ _ _.

6. I can _ _ _ _ very high.

7. I want to see the _ _ _ _ _ at the zoo.

8. The baby looks _ _ _ _ _ _.

9. I stuck a _ _ _ _ _ on and posted it.

10. Push it carefully over the _ _ _ _.

Read the text below highlight the mp words.

The Chump

The Chump lives in a swamp. It looks a bit like a dog. Its body is plump and round. It looks bumpy. There is a hump on his back. The Chump's head is small with two small bumps for ears. His legs and arms are short, like stumps.

Draw the Chump below. Use the checklist to help.

Checklist √			
swamp		small head	
plump body		2 bumps for ears	
bumpy body		legs like stumps	
hump on back		arms like stumps	

mp Dictation Sentences

1. The <u>chimp</u> <u>stamps</u> his foot.
2. You can <u>bump</u> your car on a <u>ramp</u>.
3. The <u>lamp</u> in <u>camp</u> helps me to see.
4. Don't <u>bump</u> into the <u>plump</u> man.
5. A <u>lump</u> does not look like a <u>hump</u>.

Instructions for dictation sentences

1. Read the sentence aloud to the learner(s)
2. Learner(s) repeat sentence back to you
3. Learner(s) write full sentence in their book
4. Continue until all 5 sentences complete
5. Learner finds and highlights all words containing target phoneme
6. Teacher marks learner out of 10

belt

melt

bolt

felt

salt

tilt

wilt

kilt

spilt

quilt

Name the picture

Circle the word that names the picture.

stilts pilt belt	felt gelt melt	tilt bilt quilt
melt felt prilt	bolt milt tilt	pult salt stilts
walt melt bolt	prilt wilt felt	selt kilt salt
belt salt gelt	bolt spilt slilt	halt gult bolt

Extension

Can you circle all the made up words? There is one for each picture.

Test Sheet

Fold your test sheet along the lines.
Write the word next to each picture, then check your spelling by unfolding the sheet.

Picture	Write word	Check correct spelling
		salt
		felt
		tilt
		wilt
		spilt
		quilt
		kilt
		belt
		melt

belt	
melt	
bolt	
salt	
felt	

tilt	
wilt	
spilt	
quilt	
kilt	

Silly sentences

Read each sentence. Then replace the underlined word with a rhyming word that makes sense. The word will end with lt.

1. The man has a <u>quilt</u> on.

2. The flower has started to <u>tilt.</u>

3. Look how the train <u>wilts</u> on the track.

4. The boy <u>tilt</u> his drink.

5. I made the picture with <u>belt</u>.

6. She put <u>bolt</u> on my chips.

7. At home I have a <u>kilt</u> on the bed.

8. Soon the snow will <u>felt</u>.

9. I need a <u>melt</u> for my trousers.

10. A <u>salt</u> is a metal bar or pin.

Read the text below highlight the lt words.

Scotland

In Scotland it is cold in the winter. In the winter months Scots bolt their doors, light their fires and sleep under lots of quilts.

The snow and ice in Scotland stays on the ground longer. This wilts the plants. Cars on ice must stop slowly and not with a jolt, as this could make them slip. Tilting your car on ice is not safe.

Scots sometimes put down salt on the paths to melt the ice and make it safe to walk. Most Scots are very glad when the snow melts and at last the spring starts.

lt Dictation Sentences

1. Gran made a <u>quilt</u> from <u>felt</u>.
2. The sun makes plants <u>tilt</u> and <u>wilt</u>.
3. The man has a red <u>belt</u> on his <u>kilt</u>.
4. <u>Salt</u> helps to <u>melt</u> snow.
5. Dad <u>spilt</u> his drink on the <u>bolt</u>.

Instructions for dictation sentences

1. Read the sentence aloud to the learner(s)
2. Learner(s) repeat sentence back to you
3. Learner(s) write full sentence in their book
4. Continue until all 5 sentences complete
5. Learner finds and highlights all words containing target phoneme
6. Teacher marks learner out of 10

milk

talk

walk

bulk

folk

silk

chalk

yolk

sulk

stalk

mi_ _		Add "lk" to each word.
si_ _		
cha_ _		
su_ _		
ta_ _		
fo_ _		
yo_ _		
sta_ _		
bu_ _		
wa_ _		

_ _ lk	
_ _ lk	
_ _ _lk	
_ _ lk	
_ _ lk	
_ _ lk	
_ _ lk	
_ _ _ lk	
_ _ lk	
_ _ lk	

Add the beginning to each "lk" word.

Noughts and Crosses

Make sure you read the word underneath before you draw your nought or cross.

sulk	folk	chalk
milk	talk	walk
stalk	bulk	yolk

Silly sentences

Read the caption. Draw the picture. Then write the caption underneath.

1. An egg yolk taking a walk	2. A milk jug in a sulk.	3. A flower with a bulky stalk.
4. Folk talking to chalk.	5. Folk dressed in silk.	6. A bulk sale of milk.

Silly sentences

1. An egg _ _ _ _ taking a _ _ _ _.

2. A _ _ _ _ jug in a _ _ _ _.

3. A flower with a_ _ _ _y _ _ _ _ _.

4. _ _ _ _ talking to _ _ _ _ _.

5. _ _ _ _ dressed in _ _ _ _.

6. A _ _ _ _ sale of _ _ _ _.

Ik Cloze Exercise

Choose words from below to fill the gaps.

1.   Have a glass of _ _ _ _.

2.   The pretty dress was made of _ _ _ _.

3.   Pick up the phone and _ _ _ _ to me!

4.   The _ _ _ _ _ of the flower is bent.

5.   It's cheaper to _ _ _ _ buy.

6.   It's a long _ _ _ _ from here to town.

7.   Jim is cross and is having a _ _ _ _.

8.   I like to eat egg _ _ _ _.

9.   Teachers used to use _ _ _ _ _.

10.   Some _ _ _ _ will do anything for money.

Read the text below highlight the lk words.

What a bad start!

Jim got up at six. No one was awake. He got some milk to drink. He wanted an egg. Oops! He bumped the eggs on the bulky milk carton. Egg yolk and milk spilt all over the floor. Mum was cross. Jim walked off in a sulk. When Jim came back they had a talk. "What a bad start to the day!" said Mum, as she gave him a hug.

Now answer these questions

1. What did Jim want to eat and drink?

_____

2. What spilt on the floor?

_____

3. Who was cross?

_____

4. What did Mum do when Jim came back?

_____

Extension –
Write a sentence using the words: milk, walk, bulky

lk Dictation Sentences

1. Sir gets his <u>chalk</u> in <u>bulk.</u>
2. <u>Milk</u> and <u>yolk</u> are good for you.
3. The new <u>folk</u> are in a <u>sulk.</u>
4. We will <u>walk</u> and <u>talk.</u>
5. That plant <u>stalk</u> feels like <u>silk.</u>

Instructions for dictation sentences

1. Read the sentence aloud to the learner(s)
2. Learner(s) repeat sentence back to you
3. Learner(s) write full sentence in their book
4. Continue until all 5 sentences complete
5. Learner finds and highlights all words containing target phoneme
6. Teacher marks learner out of 10

Triple Blends

spl

splash

split

splosh

splay

splint

splice

splatter

splodge

splendid

splurge

Tracking

Find the hidden words below. Each word is written only once.

1. splash
2. splatter
3. split
4. splay
5. spleen
6. splice
7. splendid
8. splurge
9. splint
10. splodge

1. Ighsplashwowsacasvfefvb

2. wdcascfvfswesplatterfv

3. splitrvbvghngpeggfvsza

4. czfvdbsplaynvzdfwebvzd

5. fvztencdavfbspleenk,jjk

6. vncbxzvtthprwdqfsplice

7. FGFsplendidGBFVDCSZC

8. fVZDBEDdfsplurgefvdcY

9. splintfdvdfzsznetxvbgvf

10. dzc\splodgemkmjhngcleg

Cross the river

Who can cross the river first? Use a dice to see how many steps you can take. For each step you take you must read the word on the stone correctly.

Extension: Colour code the blends (sp, sl, and spl)

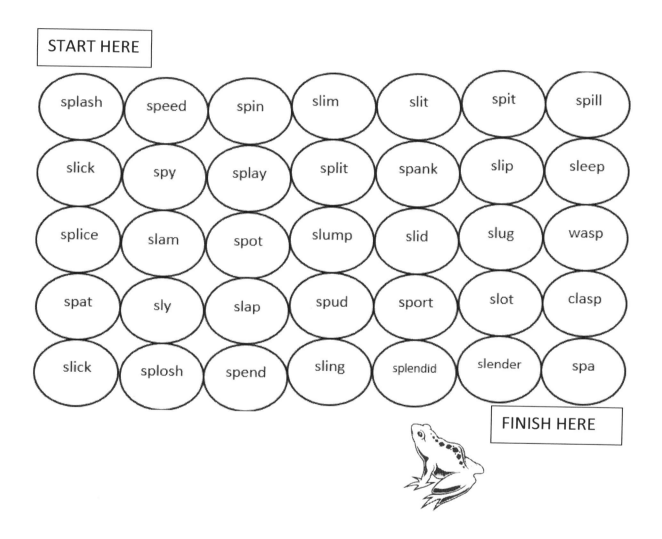

START HERE

splash	speed	spin	slim	slit	spit	spill
slick	spy	splay	split	spank	slip	sleep
splice	slam	spot	slump	slid	slug	wasp
spat	sly	slap	spud	sport	slot	clasp
slick	splosh	spend	sling	splendid	slender	spa

FINISH HERE

Note: This activity works best when enlarged to A3

227

Colour code these spl sentences to match the beginning of each sentence with the end

The dog landed in the water	and now it's in a **splint.**
My pencil has **split**	**splay** its wings.
Oh no! I've got a big	so could I have one of yours please?
Len broke his arm	**splodge** on my shirt.
Just watch that bird	with a big **splash.**

Read this text and highlight the spl words

Splodge's Splash

Splodge, the bird, had been sick. He had broken and split his wing and needed a splint. Now he was better and needed to be set free.

Splish splash splosh! Splodge landed splendidly in the water. Now he would fly. There was a small splatter as Splodge splayed his wings and flew away for good.

The bird's name is _ _ _ _ _ _ _.

Extension

Write a sentence using the words below

splash   split   splendid

strop

strap

strip

stray

street

strong
straw
strict
strain
strand

strop	
strap	
strip	
stray	
street	

strong	
straw	
strict	
strain	
strand	

str

Draw lines to match the words and pictures.

strand   straw   strap   strict   strain

street   strip   strop   strong   stray

Add "str" to complete each word.
Then fold the grey bit and have a go at spelling them on your own.

_ _ _ ip		_ _ _ _ _
_ _ _ ap		_ _ _ _ _
_ _ _ eet		_ _ _ _ _ _
_ _ _ and		_ _ _ _ _
_ _ _ ict		_ _ _ _ _
_ _ _ ay		_ _ _ _ _
_ _ _ ong		_ _ _ _ _
_ _ _ op		_ _ _ _ _
_ _ _ aw		_ _ _ _ _
_ _ _ ain		_ _ _ _ _ _

Silly sentences

Read each sentence. Then replace the underlined word with a rhyming word that makes sense.

1. The boy had a <u>mop</u> because he couldn't play.

2. I drink my drink with a <u>paw</u>.

3. The <u>fleets</u> in town are busy.

4. A <u>band</u> of hair is in my face.

5. The <u>map</u> of my shoe is broken.

6. That big man looks very <u>long.</u>

7. The teacher is <u>tricked</u>.

8. I have a <u>brain</u> on my arm.

9. Our dog used to be a <u>pray</u>.

10. I read a cartoon <u>drip</u>.

Read this text and highlight the str words

Mrs Strong is a teacher. She has streaky hair. It hangs in strands that look like straw. She slicks it back, and puts the stray strands behind her ears.

Mrs Strong wears a dress which goes straight down to her feet. On her feet are boots with big straps.

She is strict at school and sometimes has a strop. She says it's the strain of school. After school Mrs Strong helps in the Strange Street home for strays.

Are there any new str words in here? List them below.

1.

2.

3.

4.

Now draw and label Mrs Strong

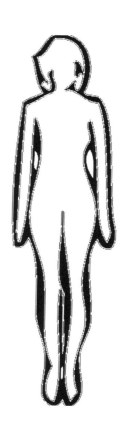

str Dictation Sentences

1. There is a <u>stray</u> <u>strand</u> of <u>straw.</u>
2. That man is having a <u>strop</u> in the <u>street.</u>
3. Mrs <u>Strong</u> is <u>strict.</u>
4. I will draw a <u>strip.</u>
5. There is a <u>strain</u> on my <u>strap.</u>

Instructions for dictation sentences

1. Read the sentence aloud to the learner(s)
2. Learner(s) repeat sentence back to you
3. Learner(s) write full sentence in their book
4. Continue until all 5 sentences complete
5. Learner finds and highlights all words containing target phoneme
6. Teacher marks learner out of 10

sh

shop

shut

ship

shell

shot

bush
flash
rush
wash
smash

Sorting exercise

Cut the words below out and stick them into the 2 boxes.

shot	mash	wash
ship	shell	shop
bush	hush	lush
flash	shin	flush
sham	shut	rush

sh at beginning of word	sh at end of word

Extension

Can you think of any more sh words that would fit in? Add them to the boxes.

Memory Test

Try to learn the list of words below. Then write as many of them as you can into the boxes.

sh at beginning of word   *sh at end of word*

ship   wash

shot   bush

shell   flash

shut   rush

shop   smash

sh at beginning of word	sh at end of word
1.	1.
2.	2.
3.	3.
4.	4.
5.	5.

Extension: Write down any more words you can remember from the sorting exercise

Connect 3. Use counters. To place a counter on a word the learner must read it correctly. The first learner to get 3 counters in a row wins.

smash	wash	**sheep**	brush
ship	**show**	shell	vanish
push	flash	**fresh**	punish
rush	mesh	**bush**	finish
hush	FLUSH	sham	*smash*

Read each sentence, then and write the correct sh word in the gap below. Use the pictures to help.

1. He _ _ _ _ the winning goal.

2. The snail has a _ _ _ _ _.

3. My front garden has a _ _ _ _.

4. My camera has a _ _ _ _ _.

5. Can you see the _ _ _ _ in the sea?

6. The man _ _ _ _ with his gun.

7. _ _ _ _ the door!

8. The glass fell with a _ _ _ _ _ _.

9. I am in a _ _ _ _

   because I am late.

Now make up a sentence yourself, using these words

shop   shut   rush

244

Read the poem below and highlight all words containing 'sh'.

Shush!

Shh!

Don't crash,

Or the thrush will fly off

From the bush

With shy flight

Of its wings.

Don't splash,

Or smash

Or the silver cat

Will go in a flash.

Hush!

If you rush

They will vanish

Before they have

Finished.

sh Dictation Sentences

1. He <u>shut</u> the door with a <u>smash.</u>
2. Pat can <u>wash</u> her <u>shell.</u>
3. That <u>flash</u> is from a <u>ship</u>.
4. The man <u>shot</u> at the <u>bush</u>.
5. Tim will <u>rush</u> to the <u>shop</u>.

Instructions for dictation sentences

1. Read the sentence aloud to the learner(s)
2. Learner(s) repeat sentence back to you
3. Learner(s) write full sentence in their book
4. Continue until all 5 sentences complete
5. Learner finds and highlights all words containing target phoneme
6. Teacher marks learner out of 10

cheek

chip

chest

chair

lunch

much

such

bench

child

chop

ch word search

Find 9 words with the blend ch in the word search below. Write each word beneath.

```
C   H   O   P   H   Y
H   C   S   U   C   H
I   H   C   H   I   P
L   I   L   C   T   C
D   P   M   U   C   H
Y   C   H   I   N   I
C   H   A   I   R   L
C   H   E   E   K   L
```

1. C H _ _   2. C H _ _ _

3. CH _ _ _   4. C H _ _

5. _ _ C H   6. C H _ _ _

7. _ _ C H   8. C H _ _

9. CH _ _ _

Extension: Solve the riddle to find the missing word from the Word Cards...

It can be a part of the body or a place to put treasure...... It is a ch _ _ _ !

ch Cloze Exercise

Choose words from below to fill the gaps.

1. On Friday lunch is fish and _ _ _ _s.

2. Fred will _ _ _ _ the tree down.

3. I sat down on a _ _ _ _ _.

4. I had chips for _ _ _ _ _.

5. A young person is called a _ _ _ _ _.

6. There is a _ _ _ _ _ wind today.

7. Sarah blushed and got red _ _ _ _ _s.

8. I have food on my _ _ _ _.

9. My birthday was _ _ _ _ a good day.

10.   Sam didn't eat _ _ _ _ lunch.

lunch	chin	such
child	chips	chill
cheek	much	chop
	chair	

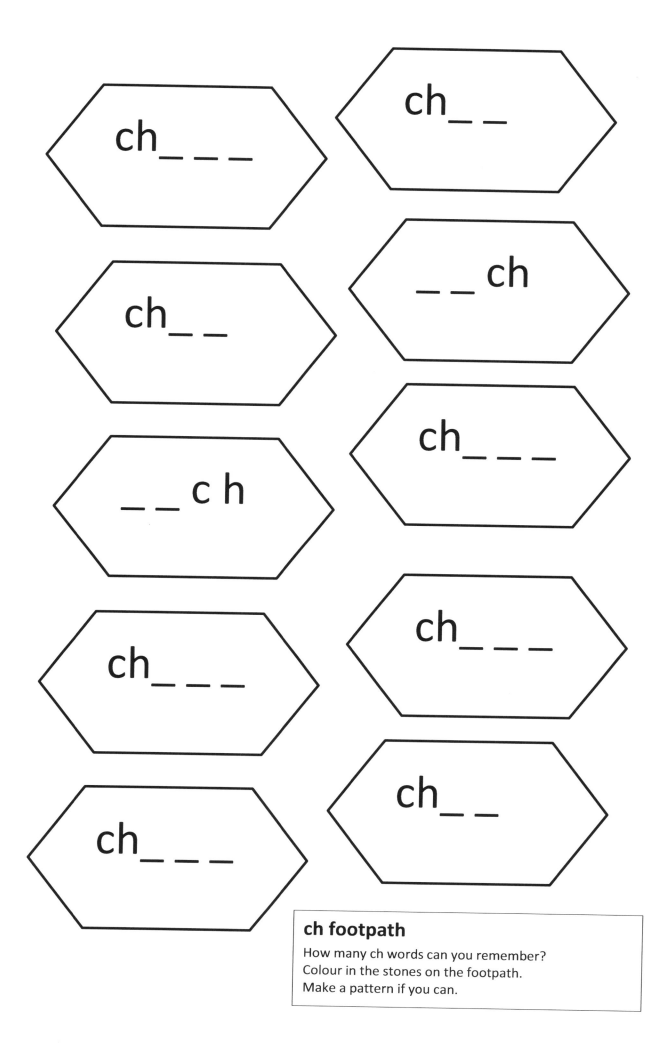

ch_ _ _

ch_ _

ch_ _

_ _ ch

_ _ c h

ch_ _ _

ch_ _ _

ch_ _ _

ch_ _ _

ch_ _

ch footpath

How many ch words can you remember?
Colour in the stones on the footpath.
Make a pattern if you can.

Read this text and highlight the ch words

The Child from China

The child has long dark hair and such big brown eyes. She has red cheeks and cherry red lips. The child has chocolate on her chin. She wears a chain around her neck. The child from China does not speak much English.

Now draw and label the Child from China.

ch Dictation Sentences

1. The <u>child</u> sits on a <u>chair</u>.
2. We need to <u>chop</u> up the <u>chips</u>.
3. Jane's <u>cheeks</u> are red from the <u>chill</u>.
4. I have <u>such</u> a bad <u>chest</u>.
5. You don't have m<u>uch</u> food on your <u>chin</u>.

Instructions for dictation sentences

1. Read the sentence aloud to the learner(s)
2. Learner(s) repeat sentence back to you
3. Learner(s) write full sentence in their book
4. Continue until all 5 sentences complete
5. Learner finds and highlights all words containing target phoneme
6. Teacher marks learner out of 10

tick

neck

pack

lock

luck

block

stuck

brick

stick

clock

Sorting exercise

Cut the words below out and stick them into the correct boxes.

tick	neck	pack
lock	block	stuck
brick	stick	clock
luck	deck	snack

ack

uck

ick

eck

ock

Can you think of any more ck words that would fit in? Add them to the boxes.

Memory test

Try to learn the words below, then write as many as you can into the boxes.

tick   neck   pack
lock   block   stuck
brick   stick   clock
luck   deck   snack

ack

_ _ _ _

_ _ _ _ _

uck

_ _ _ _

_ _ _ _ _

ick

_ _ _ _

_ _ _ _ _

_ _ _ _ _

eck

_ _ _ _

_ _ _ _

ock

_ _ _ _

_ _ _ _ _

_ _ _ _ _

Can you think of any more ck words that would fit in? Add them to the boxes.

ck Bingo

- Make sure each learner has a bingo slip.
- Each learner should read the words on their slip out loud to check understanding.
- Teacher read out the list of words, making sure the learners check their bingo slips for each word as it is read.
- If the learner hears a word on their slip they should tick it off.
- The winner may get a line (horizontal, diagonal or vertical) or a full house.

Bingo word list:
tick, neck, pack, lock, luck, block, stuck, brick, stick, clock

clock	stuck	lock	clock
stick	block	pack	stick
brick	luck	neck	brick

tick	lock	pack	brick
stick	luck	block	clock
clock	clock	stick	stick

stuck	luck	pack	tick
block	lock	neck	clock
lock	pack	neck	tick

stuck	stuck	lock	tick
brick	block	pack	clock
stick	luck	neck	stick

ck Cloze Exercise

Choose words from below to fill the gaps

1. The _ _ _ _ is part of the body.

2. Before I go I will _ _ _ _ my bag.

3. Don't forget to _ _ _ _ the door.

4. Baby Tim plays with _ _ _ _ _s.

5. Mum's car got _ _ _ _ _ in the snow.

6. Most houses are made of _ _ _ _ _s.

7. The _ _ _ _ _shows us the time.

8. The teacher _ _ _ _s to say well done.

9. Wish me _ _ _ _ with my test.

10. Dogs like to run for a _ _ _ _ _ _

Read the text below highlight the ck words.

Rick's Holiday

Rick is going away tomorrow. He is going to Woodstock. Rick will pack shorts, t-shirts and socks into his rucksack. Rick will have a quick snack and then sleep. He will set his alarm clock for 7 o'clock.

Rick's train was at 9 o'clock. The station was only around the block. He will get there quickly if he doesn't get stuck.

Good luck Rick. Have a great time and see you when you come back!

Make a list of the ck words from the text below.
List each new word, including names and place names.

1. _ _ _ _
2. _ _ _ _ _ _ _ _ _
3. _ _ _ _
4. _ _ _ _ _
5. _ _ _ _ _ _ _ _
6. _ _ _ _ _
7. _ _ _ _ _
8. _ _ _ _ _
9. _ _ _ _ _
10.   _ _ _ _ _
11.   _ _ _ _
12.   _ _ _ _

Extension
Write below any other ck words you know

ck Dictation Sentences

1. The <u>clock</u> has a <u>tick</u>.
2. <u>Pack</u> the box and then <u>lock</u> it.
3. A <u>block</u> is like a <u>brick</u>.
4. The <u>stick</u> got me in the <u>neck</u>.
5. Just my bad <u>luck</u> to get <u>stuck</u>.

Instructions for dictation sentences

1. Read the sentence aloud to the learner(s)
2. Learner(s) repeat sentence back to you
3. Learner(s) write full sentence in their book
4. Continue until all 5 sentences complete
5. Learner finds and highlights all words containing target phoneme
6. Teacher marks learner out of 10

Printed in Poland
by Amazon Fulfillment
Poland Sp. z o.o., Wrocław